The Fortune Teller's Light

The Fortune Teller's Light

AN IMMIGRANT'S JOURNEY

Edythe Shaw

ISBN: 1979529957
ISBN 13: 9781979529952
Library of Congress Control Number: 2017917525
CreateSpace Independent Publishing Platform
North Charleston, South Carolina

To the Ones who come before us and Light our way

Table of Contents

Dedication

WE ALL STAND ON THE shoulders of those who came before us. I never had a chance to know my Grandmother Fanny, my father's mother. She died five months before I was born, in 1949. But she was something of a legend in our family—and even more so for me, since I'd never met her. At the request of her brother, she immigrated to America from a Jewish village outside of Odessa when she was still a teenager. In America she single-handedly raised six children and endured unthinkable family tragedy. Doing what she had to do to survive, she ran her own business, bootlegged in the 1920s, and participated in insurance scams during the Great Depression in the 1930s. Known as "the community soothsayer," she read tea leaves and playing cards—an art she learned from the Gypsies who lived around her home in Russia.

I was always curious about her, and I got to know her only through a few family photos that showed a woman frozen in time. My father was only thirty-two years old when she died, and I noticed that throughout his life he carried a sadness within him for the loss of his mother. He used to sing an old Irish tune to her while he was in the shower: "One bright and shining light / That taught me wrong from right / I find in my mother's eyes." Or the old American standard: "M is for the million things she taught me."

When I was a young woman in my twenties, I inherited the steamer trunk that my grandmother took with her on her journey across the ocean. As I relined the inside of the tattered trunk with fresh shelf paper, I imagined what stories it held. I was fascinated by her friendship with the Gypsies, and used to wonder what it was like for her to live among them.

I wrote this story because I wanted to meet her and bring her to life. My intention is to make sure her story is not lost, and to share it with others so that they, too, might be inspired. Although some of what I've written is my own imaginative account of my grandmother's life—in accord with the threads of her biography that I've been able to gather—her story belongs to the greater story of millions of Eastern European Jewish immigrants who came to America in the great surge between 1890 and 1924.

I dedicate this book to *all* the men and women, whatever their heritage or country of origin, who immigrated to America. They came with a determination to improve not only their own lives, but the lives of their children as well. Eager to assimilate, many made their mark in our country as outstanding musicians, thinkers, scholars, scientists, and artists of all kinds. Many others were "ordinary" men and women, unsung heroes, who undertook this journey to America and parented subsequent generations. Without them we would not be here today.

PART I

The Gypsies

It is God Who has sent you

CHAPTER 1

The Mysterious Baba Kalisara

As Fanny approached the Gypsy encampment she could see the smoke rising from the morning fires. She was looking for her dear friend, Durga. When Durga's younger brother Roman caught her eye, she asked him where to find her.

"She's in the forest gathering berries," he replied in broken Russian. "She'll be back soon. Wait here."

Fanny surveyed the Gypsy camp. There were several flatbed wagons with wood houses built on them. They were covered with wooden shakes and were parked in a circle within a clearing. Horses were roaming freely, munching grass, and shooing each other away with their necks and their snorts if one of them got too close to another's breakfast patch. There were also some young ones, sticking close to their mothers. Dogs yapped and ran between the wagons, chasing one another. Fanny noticed that her own dog, Nicola, had followed her to the camp. Nicola, a mixed breed, was running around with all the other dogs, sniffing and playing. Fanny had gotten her from the Gypsy camp the previous year.

"Go home!" shouted Fanny to Nicola.

A group of young men were playing guitars, accompanied by an accordion and a violin. The music was spirited, and it inspired a sense of freedom and longing. Gypsy women in their long colorful skirts were tending the fires and preparing a breakfast of flat bread and rabbit stew. Children were running barefoot, shouting and playing amidst the wagons. Some of the women were engaged in sewing clothes. Some of the men had set up a workshop to fashion metallic tools to sell or trade, and a few of the men were busy making violins out of spruce and maple wood. These sold for a good price in the city, as the Gypsies were known to be master craftsmen of the violin.

Fanny sat down on a log stool, where she waited for her friend Durga to return. They were going to meet with Baba Kalisara, a respected elder in the Gypsy band. From Kalisara they were learning how to tell fortunes by reading playing cards.

Fanny lived with her mama, Masha, and her papa, Abe Lusher, along with six sisters and brothers. They lived in the *Pale*, an area set aside in 1791 by Russian Tzaress Catherine the Great after she had annexed Polish and Turkish territory. The Tzaress had "inherited" numerous Jewish residents whom the Russian government didn't want and didn't know what to do with. To remedy this situation, she established areas where the Jewish people could live. This she called the *Pale of Settlement*. Very few could venture "beyond the *Pale*."

Fanny lived in a Jewish village, a *shtetl*, near the city of Odessa. Her father was a shoemaker, and her mother sewed clothes and made linen cloth from flax. Fanny was the third of seven siblings. Her sister Anna was the eldest. Next came Arthur, then Fanny, followed by her younger brothers Samuel and Joseph, and the twin girls Lilly and Lana.

Just then Fanny heard some footsteps. "Greetings Fanny," came a voice from behind.

Durga had just returned from the forest. Like Fanny, she was a young girl of fifteen. "Would you like some strawberries?" she asked, holding out her basket. Fanny grabbed a handful and thanked her.

"Come," Durga said, "Kalisara is waiting for us."

Fanny followed Durga around to the back of the wagon circle. There they found Kalisara waiting for them at a makeshift table. A deck of playing cards was laid out before her on a colorful table cloth with small sewn-in mirrors that reflected the light. Kalisara was a member of the Gypsy band. Now forty-five years old, she made her living telling fortunes to city folk with her cards. Her face had a weathered look befitting one who led a nomadic life and spent most of her time outdoors. She wore a long multi-colored floral-patterned skirt. Her blouse was white with long puffy sleeves, and over that she wore a black vest that laced up with shoestring. Wound around her greying hair she had tied a red bandana. Durga and Fanny had been studying with Kalisara for several months, and they were now familiar with the basics. They knew how to lay out the cards in the Wagon Wheel spread.

Kalisara sat in front of the deck of cards that were lying on the table. She was completely still, as if in a trance. The force of her countenance seemed to quiet Fanny's own inner chatter. They sat like that for a few minutes. Slowly, Kalisara began to speak:

"Now, we will begin. Playing cards are an ordinary everyday object, which we use in a magical way." She took a deep breath in and seemed to focus on what she was about to say. Then she continued.

"In every moment, all the forces of nature are present. They come together to form *this* time and *this* place. We collect our self and focus our mind on these coordinates of the moment. We attune our inner heart to listen to what they say. It is like tuning a guitar. Each string must be in perfect resonance with all the other strings. Otherwise, discord follows."

Fanny watched with awe as the old Gypsy's eyes began to flutter. Kalisara seemed to be looking within, all the way into the depth of her soul, even though her eyes were wide open. Fanny stared, and waited for more.

"Playing cards are tools that reveal what is before us, and are symbols of the here and now. They serve to form a vessel for this moment to unfold, just as the earth is a vessel for seeds to manifest."

A shiver ran down Fanny's spine. Her eyes were wide open, and her hair seemed to stand on end, as if some electric current had entered her body. She looked at Durga, who was equally transfixed.

"The suits are symbols of the energies of a life: the good and the bad. *Diamonds* are benevolent, and are associated with discernment, how we learn and know of things.

"*Hearts* represent our emotional life and what is dear to us.

"*Clubs* are symbols of business and money. They refer to how we sustain our lives through interaction with trade, barter, and profession. They also refer to how we obtain and use our fortune.

"*Spades* are associated with death and destruction. Even though they are associated with death, this is not always bad. There is a time for everything, and there is a time to *let go*. We let go of so many things throughout our lifetime. We let go of places as we travel and move about. We let go of friends we meet along the way: sometimes family members, and sometimes possessions. Sometimes we also have to let go of our sense of pride and self-importance. Ultimately, we have to let go of our body. Loss is not always bad. Sometimes we need to lose something in order to gain another, even better, thing. This is the natural law.

"Now we will discuss the *meaning* of the cards. The kings represent a man; and, depending on the suits of the nearby cards, that man can be beneficial—or not. The king can be the querent, or a husband, father, son, brother, lover, or perhaps a friend. If it is a king of spades, it represents a rival or widower.

"Likewise the queen represents the female querent, or wife, mother, daughter, lover, sister, or friend. The queen of spades marks a widow or rival.

"The knight of diamonds represents a hope or expectation. The knight of clubs is the querent's friend or younger relation. The knight of hearts represents a new hope or an unborn child. The knight of spades signals bad news, or simply a troublesome situation.

"These are general guidelines. All cards are elements of life, and they have the capacity to influence one another. The cards that sit next to the principal card will determine the quality, the nuance, the energetics of the meaning.

"Always be general in the reading. Do not answer specific questions that may bring alarm to the inquirer. Speak to each person gently, as if they were your own kin, which in truth they are."

Kalisara became quiet. She took two deep breaths and spoke, "Until next time. *Rum tum bi salama.* Go in peace."

Fanny looked at Durga. Her eyes were closed. Her unkempt dark hair was flowing down her shoulders and back. She slowly opened her eyes; and when their gazes met, they both understood that something had entered deep inside them. They thanked Kalisara and left.

Silently, they walked to the front of the camp. Nicola was waiting for Fanny. She was curled up on the grass with her nose against her back and her tail tucked in close.

"Come, Nicola, let's go. Good-bye, Durga," Fanny said, "until next time."

As Fanny walked silently home with Nicola by her side, she pondered the impact of the day's lesson. *The layout of the cards is just like life. We are the center of our world. There are constant influences that surround us—influences that color our experience, our family, our* friends, our community, and our country. There are many things we hold dear, and challenges we wish to keep far away. How we meet these challenges determines everything.

Fanny walked on a footpath through the woods until she came to the road. She turned right and kept on walking. A young man in a horse and wagon came by and stopped. It was Tevka, the milkman's son.

"*Shalom aleichem*. Would you like a ride back home?" he inquired in Yiddish.

"*Aleichem shalom*," Fanny replied, smiling as she greeted him.

Accepting his offer, she climbed into the front seat of the wagon, with Nicola on her lap. She had to get home now, as she had promised her mother to help with the chores. Her family lived in the poor village of Gav Gubernia, one of the many Jewish villages scattered about the region. The two kilometer ride back home took just a few minutes.

"I'm home, Mama," Fanny shouted as she got out of the wagon. "Thank you, Tevka."

Fanny ran off to find her mother, with Nicola trailing behind her. Her mother, Masha, was inside, tending to the twins.

"Fanny, I'm so glad you returned," her mother greeted her in Yiddish. "Your father went to the market to sell shoes and linen. Joe and Samuel are with him. Arthur is studying Torah at the *yeshiva*. Anna can watch the twins and cook the noon meal while we go to gather flax."

Lilly and Lana were six years old and still rambunctious. "Fanny!" they shouted, and they ran to jump up and hug her. "Tell us a story, please!" they pleaded. She hugged them back.

"Okay. Come sit next to me." Lilly snuggled up to Fanny on her right side and Lana on her left.

"Once upon a time," she began, "there was a young woodpecker, and his name was Joey." The girls giggled with delight and anticipation.

"Joey was hungry, and so he went out looking for grubs to eat. He flew to a pine tree and started to peck at the wood. 'Knock, knock, knock,' he sounded with his beak. He couldn't find any grubs, so after a few minutes he left that tree and flew to a fir tree. 'Knock, knock, knock,' he sounded with his beak. After a few minutes he left that tree and flew to a birch tree. Again 'knock, knock, knock,' and again he could find no grubs. So he kept flying from tree to tree to tree. Finally, he came to a part of the forest where he heard the steady knocking of a grandfather woodpecker. He flew close and saw the grandfather eating a hardy lunch.

'O Grandfather,' Joey complained, 'I have been flying from tree to tree to tree. I am so hungry, and you have found a feast.'

'Joey,' Grandpa explained, 'you've got to be patient and keep pecking on one tree until you penetrate the outer bark. The grubs are inside the bark of the tree, not on the surface. The lesson is: Don't give up so fast! You've got to focus and remain steady in your search to go deeper to find the hidden treasure.'"

"Oooh," exclaimed Lilly and Lana.

"That's my story. I have to help Mama with the flax now. Love you, girls! I will tell you another story later. You watch Nicola."

"Okay," they said. "Come, Nicola!" And the three of them ran outside.

Mama and Fanny walked on the footpath to the bank of the nearby river where the flax grew wild. The river was wide at this point and flowed behind the village. The water was clear and cool. Fanny could see small schools of fish swimming around near the surface. Two turtles were sunning themselves on the rocks in the middle of the river, their heads and legs sticking out of their shells. Bright blue-green dragonflies skimmed the surface of the water, looking for smaller bugs to eat. A deer and two fawns were drinking water on the farther bank across the river. The little fawns still had their spots.

After their drink they followed their mother back into the forest. Birds were singing their hearts out in the tree branches above. Fanny recognized the calls of a nearby nuthatch. A blue jay caught her attention as it swooped from one branch to another, and she could hear the distant tapping sound of a lone woodpecker.

Next to the riverbank was a large patch of flax that stretched for a long way. The bright blue flowers were standing upright in the heat of the sun, which cast light and shadow as it shone through the bushes and trees. Fanny began the task of gathering the flowers. Masha helped her carefully select the best flax stalks and tie them in two bundles. When they were done, they walked home together, each carrying a bundle of flax on their shoulders.

In the garden behind the house was a storeroom where Masha kept a wooden tub filled with water. She placed the freshly gathered bundles of flax in the tub and left them there to soak for a few days. Later, Mama would take the flax out of the tub and spread the stalks outside on the ground to dry. After a few days drying outside, the flax would be brought into the storeroom and spread on the floor. When the flax was completely dry, Mama would take a bunch of the stalks and thrash them against a wide board that had a lot of fine nails protruding from it. She would run the stalks through the nails, first one end and then the other, until the flax became thoroughly separated into rough strands of fiber. She would then sort and pick out the finer fibers, manipulating them in her hands until the fibers became fluffy, like cotton batten.

Once the fibers became fluffy, they needed to be spun into thread. In the evenings, and whenever Mama had spare time, she would take a big wad of the fluffy fibers and wrap it around the mast—a smooth stick that was attached to a wooden stool made for that purpose. There was always fiber to spin. First she would moisten her fingers with saliva and pull some of the linen fibers from the mast with her right hand, twisting the fibers into thread. The thread from the right hand was quickly transferred to a spindle that she held in her left hand. She was constantly turning the spindle with her left hand, to wind around it the thread that she was creating with her right hand. In this way Masha made linen thread, which could then be made into cloth.

One of the important uses of linen in the *shtetl* was to make the table cloths that would be used for Sabbath dinner. Anna had learned to weave the threads into cloth on the loom. Once the cloth was made, she would sew the linen into Sabbath table cloths. Fanny knew how to finish the edges by making lace with thread, and she knew how to embroider the linen. Together they made fine Sabbath cloths that fetched a good price in the marketplace.

That evening, Papa and the boys returned from the village market. They had a successful day, selling many pairs of shoes and linen cloth. Merchants from five surrounding villages would gather twice a week in a village square designed for the market, where they would buy and sell their wares. Men and boys would arrive in their horse-drawn flatbed wagons, upon which they would set up their storefronts. The streets were made of cobblestone, and the market was a lively, dusty, and noisy place. Squawking animals were everywhere. The chickens clucked and pecked on the ground. The lambs bleated and jumped up and down anxiously, while the cows and calves stuck together in quiet anticipation. Some of the men had caught fish in nearby ponds and rivers to sell in the market. The dairymen sold butter, cream, and fresh milk. When Papa brought home milk, Mama would make sour cream and cottage cheese for the blintzes. Some of the vendors sold fruits and vegetables, as well as grains, beans, salt, and spices. Tonight, Papa brought home some cabbage for Anna to make a favorite dish: stuffed cabbage.

Anna and Fanny helped prepare the dinner. They had been waiting for Papa and the boys to come home from the market so they could all eat together. Sometimes Mama would trade cloth, and yesterday she had traded some linen for three chickens. Tonight she prepared one of them for dinner, saving the other two for the Sabbath meal. She asked her daughters to prepare the chicken for cooking. Fanny's job was to catch the chicken as it fluttered and ran around the fenced-in yard. Anna's job was to kill it and pluck it. Mama then made soup for dinner.

Anna cooked some of the cabbage Papa brought home, and also baked cornbread with onion. She was a good cook. A pretty girl of marriageable age, she helped in so many ways, such as watching the younger children, weaving cloth on the loom, and sewing. Mama and Papa were looking for a suitable match for her. They were thinking about the tailor's son, Martin.

Martin was strong, and was a good student at the yeshiva. Anna was happy at the thought of starting her own home. If all parties agreed, the marriage might take place in the fall. Fanny knew she'd be next. She was a little apprehensive, for she wasn't ready to leave her family just yet.

Her older brother, Arthur, was almost seventeen. He was tall and had auburn curly hair that stuck out from his *yarmulke*, the skull cap. He wore the *payot*, the side curls of orthodox Jewish boys, and spent his days at the yeshiva, learning Hebrew and studying the Torah. Arthur was a good son. He did some woodworking, and he knew how to tend to the horses. He also helped Papa in the shop, tanning hides and conditioning the leather needed to make and repair shoes and boots.

He loved Fanny and enjoyed teasing her just a little. His sisters also loved him dearly. On his first day of school they had presented him with a yarmulke they had made together. Anna had sewn the cap out of a dark blue felt, and Fanny had embroidered the Star of David on the top of it.

Life was not easy for the Jewish people in the *shtetls* of Eastern Europe. Sharing a sense of destiny, they were bound by a common culture, language, and firm spiritual ties that revolved around the Synagogue. They were thus a tight-knit community of spirit as well as of kindred belief. But as a society within Russia, the Jews were impoverished and imperiled. They had long been denied access to public education and were not allowed to trade freely. And since they had to make everything for themselves, their lives involved a constant effort for survival.

There had always been a lot of harassment of these communities. Throughout the centuries there had been worse times as well as better times. But since Tzar Alexander II was assassinated in 1881, there was a major shift in the treatment of the Jews by the new Tzar, Alexander III. Antisemitism was the order of the day. Young boys were forced to serve in the Tzar's army, and new proclamations and actions against the Jews, called *pogroms,* came forward on a regular basis. It was now 1899, and the pogroms kept getting worse.

The Gypsies, who lived among the Jews, were also allowed to wander in the Pale of Settlement; but, unlike the Jews, they were permitted to go to the city for work. The Gypsy women would tell the fortunes of the Russian ladies, either by reading their palms or by using cards or tea leaves. They were also employed as domestics in some households. Dressed in brightly colored costumes, they often danced to the music of the Gypsy men, who entertained the city dwellers by playing in the local clubs and on the streets. The men were not only renowned musicians, but were also very good horsemen, and for that reason were frequently employed to take care of the horses. Thus were Gypsies tolerated, as a general rule, and the Russians allowed them a little more freedom of movement within the country than they did the Jews.

CHAPTER 2

A Voyage with No Return

THE FOLLOWING WEEK, DURGA CAME to Fanny's door. "Come Fanny," she said excitedly, "Kalisara is asking for us."

Fanny grabbed her shawl and ran out of the house, following Durga down the path. Durga was a young girl, just beginning to blossom into womanhood. She had dark, smooth skin. Her cheeks were always a little bit dusty, her long shiny hair a little bit unkempt, her colorful clothes a little tattered. Durga had brought her horse, a fine brown mare named Manu. Fanny hopped on Manu behind Durga, and they sped off down the road towards the Gypsy camp. She held on tight to Durga's waist as they galloped along.

After traveling for a while, Fanny noticed a patch of echinacea purple cone flowers at the side of the road. She especially admired the color of the downward facing petals, and made a mental note to come back to dig up the echinacea root: *Mama could make a tincture from the root to use for medicine to take when we get sick.*

When they arrived at the camp, Fanny noticed a lot of activity. Men and women were packing the wagons. "What's going on?" Fanny asked.

"A small group of us are leaving for Brody next week," Durga replied. "The men will be trading some horses and tending to others. Some of the men and women will be playing music and dancing at the *kabaks*, the local bars in the city. Then we will return."

Kalisara was waiting around the back of the camp for the girls to arrive. She wore a long, bright-green, ruffled skirt with colored lace sewn into it. From under the edges of the red scarf she was wearing, wisps of her curly salt-and-pepper-colored hair fell upon her forehead. As there was still a morning chill in the air, she had wrapped a knitted shawl around her shoulders.

Kalisara sported a big smile when she saw Fanny and Durga approach. "*Devlay sah ah veelan*, It is God who has sent you," she greeted them in her native Romani language.

In front of Kalisara, on her card reading table, she had placed a glass vase of wild flowers: white daisies, purple lupine, shooting stars, and other delights of the meadow. Incense smoke was rising from the burning sage she had lit in a round clay bowl at one end of the table. The smoke wafted up and merged in the currents of the wind. The scent was woody and earthy, giving an air of inspiration and hope. A bowl of freshly picked berries was perched on the edge of the table. It was as if she was showing the girls how to set the mood in the card reading session, engaging the five senses of smell, sight, taste, touch, and hearing—while also calling forth the five elements of earth, fire, water, air, and space.

"Please sit," she beckoned the girls.

Kalisara closed her eyes for a few minutes. She seemed to go deep inside. Fanny spontaneously closed her eyes as well, and felt a wave of energy course through her from the top of her head to the base of her spine. Her breath became still. Kalisara began to speak:

"When clients come to you, seeking advice, know that their hearts are open to you and what you bring. Be gentle with the heart.

The mind, however, will be fluctuating. You must learn how to read the mental makeup of the person before you. Some people will be agitated, some will be in grief. Some will be anxious, and some will be hopeful. Some will be eager to receive direction for a question in their heart. But all will listen carefully to you.

"Over time you will learn to read the body language of those who seek your guidance. You will learn to assess their mental condition. Adjust your forecast accordingly. A fidgety person may be nervous or anxious; someone clutching their heart may be hopeful. Look at the muscles of the body. Are they relaxed, or tense? Are there tears in the eyes? Is the smile forced, or is it genuine? Are the cheeks red, or pale? What clothes do they wear? Are they new, or worn out? All these observations are indications of a person's readiness for what you are about to unfold before them.

"Never say too much or too little. Do not be specific in dates, time, or people. Keep the forecast neutral and general. If there is a question about a love interest, indicate to the client that they will meet a special man or woman. If there is a question regarding money or finances, do not elaborate where the money will come from. Hint at several possibilities of acquisition, based on the layout of the cards. Be especially gentle in interpreting tragedy cards, only hinting at possible outcomes. Avoid answering direct questions, and never ask questions of your client. Give enough indications to allow the client to formulate for themselves the answers they seek.

"Trust your inner self to match and interpret the cards as they are laid out. Watch how the client shuffles the deck. Is their mood triumphant, or hesitant? Instruct them to concentrate on the subject for which they are seeking help.

"Learn to be a good observer of human behavior. Enter a state of witness consciousness when interpreting the cards. The layout of the cards shows how different elements of a person's life relate to each other, indicating a predictable outcome. Enter inside the message of the cards, and become a witness to the unfoldment of these elements that come into play by their placement in the spread.

"Fanny, let us now do a sample reading for you. Shuffle the deck and choose a principal card that represents you."

Fanny opened her eyes and took the deck of cards in her hands. She felt the weight of the cards and the gravity of the moment. After taking two long breaths, she drew the queen of hearts as her principal card. She shuffled the deck several times, dropping the cards slowly from her right hand to her left. Then she placed them on the table in front of Kalisara.

Kalisara cut the pack into two, and joined the cards again. Then she laid out the top two cards to the right and to the left of the principal card, the queen of hearts. After that she took two more cards, placing them first below, then above the queen. To fill in the spaces, four more cards were laid down, angled carefully between the four central cards. Finally, eight more cards were placed, forming a circle around the center cards. This created an image of a spoked wheel— called the Wagon Wheel spread.

The Wagon Wheel Spread

Kalisara studied the cards and their relationships to one another. She told Fanny she would be successful in business and would have a large family of her own. Trouble would arise with her husband, and an upset would occur with one daughter. She would work hard, while leading a mostly comfortable life. Many people would consult her.

Then Kalisara noticed the three of spades next to the six of spades, surrounded by the knight of spades in the position of the immediate future. She remained silent for a moment, as if hesitating to articulate. Then slowly and carefully, she spoke: "There will arise concern with your brother, and a voyage with no return is in your future."

Fanny was taken aback. Kalisara's words pierced her heart like a sword. She didn't know yet what to make of this forecast. She did not doubt the authenticity of what Kalisara saw in the cards. It was only that she wasn't ready for such an event to take place. Could she leave Mama and Papa and all her sisters and brothers, and Nicola? It was unthinkable. How could she leave her friend Durga, and all her aunts, uncles, and cousins? It was unfathomable. And yet, something inside told her it was inevitable. She knew the neighbor's son had to leave for America last spring to avoid being conscripted into the Tzar's army. She knew his mother missed him every day. She'd heard of people who had left the village—but *she* couldn't. Not her, not now. She quickly silenced these thoughts and tucked them back into the shadows of her mind, into the part that forgets: the part that veils and covers what may be.

Fanny smiled, "Thank you, Kalisara. It was helpful to be the recipient of the card reading. It's important to know what it's like to be in the shoes of the querent. It will help me tremendously. And now I must go. I promised to help Mama and Anna with the chores."

"*Atoh me develesa*, Stay with God," Kalisara spoke as she ended the session.

"I can take you home," Durga said. She led Fanny to where Manu was grazing in the forest behind the camp. "Hop up."

The two girls mounted the horse. Slowly Durga turned her around, and they started back down the path. "Please," Fanny asked

Durga, "Can we stop by the echinacea in the meadow to dig up the root? I'd like to take it to Mama."

"Sure," answered Durga. "I will bring my small shovel with us." Durga hopped off and ran to her wagon to get it. She came back, and soon they were sauntering down the road.

After a while they came upon the bright-purple and pinkish-purple cone flowers shining in the meadow. "There they are," Fanny shouted into Durga's ear.

"Whoa," whispered Durga to Manu, who then came to a halt. The girls jumped off and started to dig up the roots and put them in a cloth bag. Manu was content to graze in the meadow.

"Will you be going to Brody?" asked Fanny.

"Yes, I'll be going with Mama and Papa. Papa has a customer there. He helps with the horses. He breaks them in and helps with grooming and shoeing. Mama dances in the streets with the musicians, and I circle the crowd with a cup, asking for tips."

"What's it like in Brody?" Fanny asked.

"It's a big city, with finely dressed men and women. There are tall buildings, and on the cobblestone streets there are gas lamps. A lamplighter comes by every night to light them. There are big stables for the horses, and stores with big windows. You can even get different kinds of food at restaurants that are everywhere in the city, and there are two-storey houses painted red, brown, and yellow. It's quite lovely."

After the girls finished gathering the roots, they climbed back on Manu. Durga then dropped Fanny off at her home.

"Thank you," Fanny said, as she disappeared into the house.

"*Shalom,* Mama," she greeted, as she walked in. "I'm back to help with chores. I brought some echinacea root for you." Then Fanny noticed her mother looking worried and despondent.

"What's the matter?"

Masha spoke, "Your father and I are worried for Arthur's safety. The Russian military came by to inform us that on Arthur's next birthday, when he turns seventeen, he will be forced to join the Tzar's army and will be sent to the front lines. We've been wringing our hands and searching our hearts, discussing what to do. Your Papa has an Uncle Samuel who lives in America, and we've been in correspondence with him. We are thinking the best solution for all would be to send him to America to live with Uncle Samuel. It will be a heartbreaking parting, but he must go for his own sake, and ours."

"When would he go, Mama?"

"He will go as soon as we can arrange it."

"How will he get there?"

"We need to get him to Brody, in Austria. From there, a volunteer from the Jewish agency, the Universal Israeli Alliance, will help him to secure a ticket for a train to Hamburg. In Hamburg, our neighbor's cousin Moshe will make sure he gets a passage on a ship to America. The question is how to get him to Brody safely."

Fanny was saddened at this news. She loved her brother Arthur dearly. For a moment, she was lost in despair. After she recovered from the shock of the news, she was ready to help. She had an idea. "Durga is going with her family to work in Brody next week! They leave on the full moon night. Arthur could travel with them in the Gypsy wagon. If it is all right with you, I could ask Durga about it tomorrow."

"I don't know, Fanny. That could be risky. I will discuss it with your father and Arthur, and let you know," said Mama. "If they agree, we'll prepare Arthur for the long journey."

Arthur was just two years older than Fanny, and they had always been close. They played together when they were kids. Fanny tagged along with Arthur when he and his friends went fishing. They'd play on the riverbank, hopping over rocks and picking dandelion seeds.

They'd blow on the fluffy white seeds to see how many were left on the stem. That would determine how many children they would have, or some other childish delight. Fanny remembered when Papa built a wooden wagon for them to play with, and how Arthur took great joy in pulling Fanny all around the yard in it. The chickens would squawk and flutter to get out of the way. Arthur and Fanny liked to explore the area together. They'd run and skip down the road, laughing and chasing after each other. And one day, they came upon the Gypsy camp. That's how Fanny met Durga.

They often helped Mama with the chores. They would sweep and clean and help set the table. But of all the chores, they loved best to help her bake the challah bread. They would watch as Mama mixed and rolled out the dough. They would help her knead the bread. Then Mama would put the dough in a covered bowl on the stove, so the yeast would warm up and the bread would rise. After a few hours, when the bread had risen, Mama would shape the dough by braiding it. She would then brush the top with egg white, creating the distinctive challah shape and shiny crust. After that, she'd bake it in the hot oven. Arthur and Fanny also liked to help Mama bake noodle kugel, as well as mandelbrot—a yummy twice-baked cookie.

Arthur was one of those naturally sweet souls who were kind and respectful to everyone. In the winter, he would help the neighbors gather wood and keep the walkways clear of snow. He knew how to tend to the horses. He fed them, groomed them, and kept them warm in the barn during winter. And when the time came for him to prepare for his Bar Mitzvah, that's when he began his schooling at the yeshiva.

Arthur was a gentle soul, and as such he was not equipped to be a soldier in the army. It was known that the Jewish soldiers were not treated well. They would be poorly fed and poorly equipped. They would be made to march for days in snow or rain, and sent to the front lines. Arthur was worried. He felt intimidated at the thought of being forced to join the Tzar's army. Although he preferred to stay at home with his family, he realized how serious conscription was. In all likelihood it was a death sentence. As a Jew he would be cast into a Jewish regiment and treated with total disregard, while also not being allowed to say the prayers or light the candles. So Arthur knew he had to leave. He was both excited and scared.

Masha and Abe discussed with him how serious it was to travel. If he was stopped by the soldiers before reaching the border, they would not let him proceed. Traveling with the Gypsies in their caravan was an idea they hadn't thought of. Would it work? Gypsies had free reign of the territory, as they were always moving about and were rarely harassed or stopped by the police. That would be like trying to stop the wind.

After much discussion and thought, the plan became clear. The next morning, Mama asked Fanny to see if she could arrange for Arthur to travel to Brody with Durga and her parents in the Gypsy caravan. Fanny ran to the camp with Nicola by her side. Nicola's tail wagged from side to side, and her long ears flew back in the wind. She'd stop and sniff the ground every so often with her moist black nose. When they reached the camp, Fanny looked around for Durga. She found her by her wagon, cooking breakfast.

"Hi Fanny," she said, looking up. Durga was happy to see her. "Would you like some bean and carrot stew?"

"No thanks. I've come to ask you and your parents if my brother Arthur can travel with you to Brody. It seems he is in danger of being conscripted soon, and Mama and Papa want to send him to America, where our Uncle Samuel lives."

"Papa and Roman have gone hunting. When they come back, I'll ask him. I'm sure it will be alright. There will be many of us traveling, and one more person won't matter much."

"It may be dangerous if the police stop the wagon and find him, or if he gets caught at the border," Fanny said, with a little fear in her voice.

"Papa and the other men know the local police, and they usually let us pass without any problem. To them, we are just the crazy local Gypsies. Arthur can stay inside the wagon until we get to the border."

"Do they search the wagon at the border?" Fanny inquired.

"Not usually," replied Durga, hoping to reassure her friend, "not unless they suspect something. We leave in two days—at night, when the full moon rises. That way we arrive at the border the next day. It will take about a week to reach Brody. We're taking some young horses with us to sell, and Arthur can help with the horses once we pass the border."

Later that morning, Durga sent word that her parents, Maya and Parush, had agreed to the arrangement. Arthur was to meet the Gypsy caravan on the road in two days' time, when the full moon would be rising.

CHAPTER 3

Arthur Goes to Brody

OVER THE NEXT TWO DAYS, Mama baked for Arthur. You could see the sadness in the wrinkles around her eyes. She was apprehensive for his safety. Arthur packed all his clothes into one shabby leather suitcase that was torn a little at the edges. Mama gave him two brass candlesticks for keeping the Sabbath. Determined to make sure he would not go hungry while traveling, she packed cornbread, cheese biscuits with onion, fruit, and dried meat. Papa gave him twenty rubles for his voyage, along with a letter to give to their neighbor's cousin Moshe in Hamburg. Papa and Mama instructed him on how to watch out for thieves and pickpockets in the city, and warned him to always be vigilant.

On the full moon night, Arthur and his family met the Gypsy caravan on the road near their house. Arthur was bundled up with his coat, scarf, and gloves. He carried with him only one battered suitcase and his Bible. Wrapped up in an old scarf was Mama's care package of food that she had prepared for him to take on his journey.

Everyone was crying and hugging Arthur for the last time. Anna gave him a special embroidered yarmulke to remember her by. As the boys hugged Arthur good-bye, they were sad and a little fearful for their own future. Lilly and Lana were so small, and Arthur so tall, that they could only reach just past his knees. They hugged his legs and said, "We'll miss you." Even Nicola jumped up and put her two front paws on Arthur's leg, whimpering as if to say a sad good-bye. Mama was in tears. Papa hugged Arthur and asked him to write when he got settled. Fanny gave him a hug and a kiss. "Until we meet again," she whispered in Yiddish.

The Gypsy caravan came to a stop. There were six wagons loaded with goods to sell in the city. A few broken-in young horses were tied to the wagons to trade or to sell. Arthur got into the wagon with Durga's family. Durga's father, Parush, would be steering the horses, and her younger brother, Roman, was sitting up in the front with his father. Durga's mother, Maya, greeted Arthur and welcomed him into their wagon home.

"Click, click," Parush uttered, signaling to the horses to move, and the caravan started up again.

Arthur could hear the jangle of the harnesses mixed with the sound of the horses' hooves on the dirt road. He was a little bit excited for the adventure; and for a moment he even forgot he was leaving his family, maybe for good. Looking out of the window, in the brightness of the full moon, he could see squirrels darting about on the forest floor. As they passed by a stream, he could hear the quiet gurgling of the water flowing over the rocks. Soon they came to a small pond. Arthur noticed the light of the moon creating a long beam of light on the surface of the water. He noticed the undulating ripples created by a gentle wind. The sweet smell of fresh blossoms filled the air.

Maya spoke, "Under the floor of our wagon is a storage cabinet. If for any reason we get stopped by the soldiers, you can take refuge down there." She rolled back the rug and took up a few loose boards in the floor, exposing a small space big enough for a man to curl up into. Arthur shuddered as his reverie was brought back to the reality of the situation. Would the Gypsy caravan be stopped? What would happen if the Russian soldiers found him, a Jew, illegally leaving the country? He shuddered to think of such a thing. He had a passport, because all Russian citizens had to register with the government; but he didn't have permission to leave, and thus hadn't gotten the required exit permit stamped in his passport. Then he quickly put those thoughts to rest in the back of his mind, and settled down once again into the rhythm of the journey.

Arthur fell into a quiet slumber, as the caravan continued down the road. After some time, the horses seemed to get restless and started to whinny and snort. The dogs barked as if they sensed strangers on the road. Suddenly frightened, Arthur shook himself out of his nap, as his heart started to pound. Could these be soldiers approaching? Arthur heard howls in the distance and then knew that a pack of wolves was nearby, possibly watching the caravan for any stragglers to catch. He laughed nervously to himself and tried to settle back down in his seat, while the caravan continued on into the night.

When morning came, the caravan stopped by a small stream. The Gypsies formed a circle with the wagons. They got down from them to go into the woods to relieve themselves and to take care of the morning toiletries. The women got out the pots and pans and started fires to cook the morning meal. The children ran around. The horses were released into the forest to drink water, graze, and rest a bit. The women then boiled water for washing up before breakfast.

Arthur was reluctant to get out of the wagon. With his yarmulke and side curls he felt self-conscious, as he was apprehensive of being discovered—not by his friends, but by some strangers passing by. He asked Maya for a Gypsy bandana, which he tied around his yarmulke while tucking his *payot* behind his ears. Then he, too, went to relieve himself in the woods. When he came back to the wagon he was hungry. He grabbed one of Mama's cheese biscuits and began to eat ravenously, remembering her love and care for him. For a moment he lost himself, thinking about Mama and how much she meant to him.

After a well-needed rest, the wagons were repacked, the horses were rounded up and hitched to the reins, and the caravan set off again. The men expected to reach the border by late in the afternoon.

After many hours, the caravan stopped. Parush told Arthur that it was now time for him to get into the undercarriage storage cabinet, since they were getting close to the border. Maya rolled back the carpet and lifted the boards up to reveal the storage area. Arthur climbed into it, anxiously awaiting his fate.

Finally, after what seemed like an interminable amount of time, the wagons were stopped at the Russian border. Afraid even to breathe, Arthur held very still. Russian soldiers stood in a line, guarding the border with their rifles pointed at the travelers.

"Stop!" they commanded in Russian. There was nothing else the Gypsies could do.

"Whoa," said the wagon drivers, and the horses came to a halt.

"Get down from your wagons," they shouted. "Everyone get out of the wagons!" The men and boys hopped down from the front carriage, while the women and children got out from inside the wagons.

Django, the leader of the caravan, spoke with the Russian Captain. He knew Russian the best.

"Where are you going?" the Captain asked.

"To Brody," Django replied.

"What are you going to do there?"

"We have work to do. Our employers are waiting for us."

"What work do *you* have?" he asked sarcastically. All the soldiers were smirking—because Gypsies had a reputation for being pickpockets and thieves, and for conning good people.

Django replied with dignity, "We help with the horses—grooming, shoeing and breaking them in. We brought some young horses to sell. Some of us play music at the *kabaks* to entertain the people. We have an engagement to play music for the Mayor of Brody." Django showed him a letter of invitation from the Mayor.

"How long will you be gone? When are you coming back?"

"We expect to be back on the next full moon," Django replied.

"What are you bringing? Are you smuggling anything of value or . . . anyone?" he barked.

Django just shook his head. "Search the wagons!" the Captain shouted.

The soldiers fanned out with their rifles and entered all the wagons. They were looking for gold, or anything else of value that was not permitted to leave the country, as well as for anyone the Gypsies might be hiding. Maya and Durga got down from the wagon. Durga gave her mother a quick, anxious glance. Maya almost imperceptibly shook her head, as if to tell her daughter not to worry.

Arthur heard all the menacing dialogue between Django and the Russian Captain. His heart was pounding. When the order was given to search the wagons, Arthur thought his chest would explode. Just then he noticed that one board at the back of the storage cabinet was loose. He removed it as quietly as he could, and it seemed there was another compartment behind it that was even smaller. He quickly rolled in there. Curled up in the fetal position, he barely fit. Then, just as the soldiers were about to enter the wagon, he replaced the board.

He kept as still as he possibly could, desperately hoping not to be discovered. Spontaneously, he started to pray: *"Barukh atah Adonai, Eloheinu; Barukh atah Adonai, Eloheinu; Barukh atah Adonai, Eloheinu* . . . Blessed Art Thou, O Lord our God; Blessed Art Thou, O Lord our God."* He kept repeating the prayer over and over in his mind, silently focusing on the One Merciful God.

The heavy footsteps above him shook his whole body. He could hear the soldiers sniff and snort and carelessly move Maya and Parush's belongings all about the wagon with the butts of their rifles. Then they noticed a wrinkle in the carpet. Suspicious of something, they pulled back the carpet. Noticing the two loose boards, they pulled them up and pointed their rifles into the cabinet, certain they were going to find something or someone. Arthur inhaled, but didn't dare exhale. Durga gasped quietly. Her heart began to pound! When the soldiers looked inside the cabinet, all they found were some empty glass bottles and a few rags. Disappointed, they grunted and left the wagon. Arthur breathed a sigh of relief, but still didn't dare move until Maya gave him a signal.

"Okay," they said, stepping down from the wagon. The Captain shouted, "You may cross the border!" The soldiers opened the gate to allow the caravan to pass.

Everyone got back into the wagons. The men each climbed into their driver's seats and took the reins.

"Click, click," they signaled to the horses, and the Gypsy caravan continued down the road. Durga looked at her mom quizzically, as if to ask, *Where is Arthur?* And Maya just held her forefinger to her lips as if to say, *Hush.*

After ten kilometers they came to the border of Austria-Hungary, where Emperor Franz-Joseph was ruling. Django knew the Austrian border guards, as he had crossed over many times before. The guards stopped the wagons to chit-chat and ask the compulsory questions. Then, with a nod and a wave, they let the caravan enter the country.

Ten kilometers into Austria, Maya signaled to Arthur that it was okay to come out of his hiding place. Durga's mouth opened in amazement. She was so relieved to see Arthur. If anything had happened to him, how could she have told Fanny? It was unthinkable.

"What happened?" she asked in bewilderment. "I thought for sure the soldiers would find you!"

Arthur explained to her that once he was in the cabinet, he noticed another loose board at the side, and that behind this board was a smaller space which he rolled into just as the soldiers entered the wagon. His heart had pounded so loud he thought the soldiers would hear it. In all the excitement, Durga had forgotten about the hidden compartment.

The rest of the journey was unremarkable, and Arthur now breathed a sigh of relief.

After a few days, the caravan arrived in Brody. They stopped a couple of kilometers outside of town to set up camp. At a clearing near a stream, they again formed a circle with their wagons. The men and boys unhitched the horses to graze, drink, and rest. The women got out the pots and pans to cook and to heat up water for washing. Younger children ran around, while the older children helped with the chores. They would all go into town a little later.

Arthur washed up, ate a little, and then it was time for him to leave. He gathered up his Bible, his suitcase, and his now empty scarf, which Mama had given him for carrying the food she had prepared for him. He caressed the scarf lovingly, thinking of Mama. *"I made it, Mama!"* he said to her in his mind.

"Thank you so much, *A dank, A sheynem dank. Nais tuke, Nais tuke,*" Arthur repeated in Yiddish and Romani to Maya and Durga. He found Parush and Roman. "*A dank, Nais tuke,*" he repeated, "I couldn't have crossed the border without your help. I am forever indebted to your kindness."

"*Atsch me Devalesa,*" Maya spoke, "Be with God."

Durga and Roman hugged Arthur good-bye. "Give my love to Fanny," Arthur told Durga. "And tell her we reached Brody safely."

Arthur went to look for Django, who was tending the horses. "Thank you so much," Arthur said.

"*Rum tum bi salama*," Django spoke, "Go in peace."

Arthur took his things and started to walk into town, which was only a short distance away. It didn't take him long. Having never been in a city before, he didn't know what he'd find. Durga had described the town to him, so he had some idea of the location of the train station, the city square, the Cathedral, the Synagogue, and other landmarks. He was in Austria-Hungary now, where all the signs were in both German and Hungarian. Arthur knew Russian, Yiddish, and by now a smattering of the Gypsy tongue Romani—but he didn't know German. He quickly realized that Yiddish shared some words with German, so he knew he would be able to get by.

When Arthur entered the city, he was filled with wonder. His eyes opened wide as he stared at everything. For a moment he forgot himself, as he was fascinated by all the new sights and sounds. There were wide streets and tall buildings. There were rows of houses painted in beautiful colors. The smell of fresh baked bread and sweets wafted from the bakery. Fresh meat hung from the windows of the butcher shop. Beautiful cheeses were on display at the cheese shop. There were restaurants and bars along the streets. Everything was enchanting to his senses. Women and men were dressed in tailored clothes, and there were decorated horses and carriages. But the biggest surprise by far was to see a *horseless* carriage drive by! Arthur was amazed. He scratched his head in wonder at this, as he had never before seen or heard of such a thing.

After a while, Arthur asked a passerby in Yiddish where the Jewish Synagogue was located. The reply came in German, and he understood only half of it. Still, he kept walking in the direction pointed out to him, and soon came to the Synagogue. The office of the Universal Jewish Alliance was located at the back of the building. Arthur walked into the office, so relieved to be among kin. A man sitting behind the desk was wearing a yarmulke and sported a beard on his chin. Arthur noticed he did not have side curls. His helpful eyes were magnified behind his eyeglasses. He introduced himself as Marvin.

"*Shalom aleichem*," Arthur said.

"*Aleichem shalom,*" came the reply. "How can we help you? From where have you come?" Marvin gave a welcoming smile.

Arthur found himself relieved to finally be able to talk to someone in Yiddish. He explained everything about how the Russian soldiers had come to his parent's house, and how the decision was made for him to leave for America. He told Marvin how he had traveled with the Gypsies, and of the harrowing story of crossing the Russian border. "I was told you could help me get a train ticket to Hamburg," Arthur said. "From there I will find our neighbor's cousin, Moshe, who will help me get passage on an ocean liner to New York."

"That's good," replied Marvin. "I can put you up for the night, and tomorrow we will make sure you are on the train to Hamburg. It leaves from here at noon. Do you have a passport with you?"

"Yes," replied Arthur, "but I don't have an exit permit from Russia."

"How much money do you have with you?"

"Twenty rubles."

"That will be just enough." Looking directly into Arthur's eyes in order to convey a sense of trust, Marvin continued, "Leave your passport and money with me for the night. I will make sure you have the proper permits stamped into your passport, including your exit permit from Russia, as well as your entrance and exit permits from Austria-Hungary. I will have your rubles exchanged into Deutsche marks. It will be easier for you to change the German marks into American dollars when you arrive in New York, and you will be able to pay for your steamship passage.

"Now, do come home with me. I'll introduce you to my wife, Sylvia. We'll make sure you get a good meal and rest."

Arthur followed Marvin home, which was close by. After introducing Arthur to his wife and children, Marvin then left to finish the day's business. Sylvia showed Arthur to his room, where he could wash and rest up before his long journey to America. He soon fell into a deep, silent sleep.

After some time passed by, Arthur heard a soft knock on the door. It was Jacob, Marvin's nine-year-old son. "Sir," he said, "it's time for dinner."

Arthur got up, dusted off his clothes, combed his hair, and went for dinner. Marvin's wife had cooked brisket and cabbage rolls, with noodle kugel for dessert. It was quite a feast. Arthur ate heartily and with good manners.

"Thank you, thank you, *A dank, a dank*," Arthur said. "It was delicious. I haven't eaten like this since I left home."

After dinner, Marvin sat down in the parlor for a smoke and invited Arthur to sit with him. When he finished his cigarette, he said to Arthur, "Let's go out to the bar. I want to show you the night life of Brody."

The two men walked to the center of town. Marvin led him through the streets and lanes of the city until they came to the *Zipfer Bierhaus*, the most famous beer house in all of Brody. Arthur was hesitant. He had never been to a beer house before, and he never drank alcohol—except for a glass of wine at the Sabbath table and during Passover, and that was *only* for ritual purposes.

"Come on," encouraged Marvin, "Don't be shy. This is the night life in Brody. You will find this in America too."

Arthur entered the beer parlor. It was filled with a lot of smoke and much noise from the men who were shouting and laughing out loud. Some were rowdy and seemed erratic in their behavior. While

Marvin ordered beer, Arthur just had water. "There will be entertainment tonight!" shouted Marvin over the noise in the bar.

Just then, the musicians entered the stage and the lively music started. Arthur looked up with surprise. His Gypsy friends were playing guitar and violin and beating the tambourine. Some of the women he knew were dancing in brightly-colored costumes. They were wearing white blouses with puffy sleeves and low necklines, and colorful ribbons in their long dark hair. As they moved about on the stage, they swished their wide skirts up and down with their hands.

Waving his hands, Arthur smiled at the Gypsies, and they smiled back.

"Do you know them?" asked Marvin.

"Yes, they are from my home village. They are very kind and generous people." Arthur sat back, closed his eyes, and delighted in the music as his thoughts turned to home.

After breakfast the next morning, Arthur met Marvin at his office. Marvin gave him back his passport with the proper stamps on the pages. He also gave him thirty-three Deutsche marks, which were left over after the exchange of his rubles and after buying the ticket to Hamburg.

"Here is your train ticket. The railway station is in the center of town, where we walked last night. Good-bye and good luck. *Shalom.*"

"*Shalom,*" responded Arthur. "Thank you for your help. I am forever indebted to you."

Arthur walked to the train station with his leather suitcase, his Bible, and the scarf Mama had given him. When the train arrived, he gave his ticket to the conductor and took his seat. As the train pulled out of Brody and headed to Hamburg, Arthur felt a sigh of relief. So far, everything was going as planned. He felt lucky, and grateful for all the help he was given on his way.

Arthur looked around at his fellow passengers on the train. There were gentlemen in well-made suits and hats. The women were dressed in beautiful clothes, and the children seemed well-behaved. He noticed that not very many men had Yiddish side curls—and because he wore them, he felt a little conspicuous. He wondered if he should cut his off. He didn't want to stand out on the voyage to America.

The train pulled into Hamburg. Arthur was excited to be on this next leg of his journey. He got down from the train with his baggage in hand. The Hamburg train station was enormous, and somewhat confusing. There were multiple tracks, and people were going every which way. He found a man wearing a yarmulke and asked him in Yiddish for directions to Moshe's house. He had the address in his pocket and showed it to the man.

"I am going that way," he said. "You can come with me."

They started down the busy street, away from the train station. In 1899, Hamburg was a busy port city, much bigger than Brody. There was the hustle and bustle of the port itself, where large cargo ships were continuously being loaded and unloaded by the dockworkers. In the middle of town were big buildings and large department stores, as well as several bookstores, clothing stores, and shops of every sort. Many horseless carriages were on the street, like the one he had seen in Brody.

Arthur's new friend led him to Moshe's house. They had taken the trolley. When they arrived, Moshe opened the door with a smile. "*Shalom aleichem*," he said.

"*Aleichem shalom*," Arthur replied. He thanked his friend for escorting him to Moshe's house. Then Arthur handed Moshe the letter of introduction from Papa, explaining that they were neighbors of his cousin in Gav Gubernia and requesting him to please help his son arrange for passage to New York. Moshe was glad to help.

"Every day, there are hundreds, maybe thousands of Jews from Eastern Europe who come through Hamburg, looking for passage to America. Many young men such as yourself are taken advantage of. Innkeepers charge too much, baggage is stolen, and tickets are sold to the wrong destination. Con men, thieves, money changers, and thugs are waiting everywhere to pounce on the next victim. It is good you have come here.

"The steamship companies are requiring medical checkups before you can board the ship. This is because they would have to carry back any immigrant, free of charge, who is denied entry into the United States due to illness. When there was a fear of the plague and when outbreaks of trachoma or tuberculosis became common, there were quarantines at the docks for as long as two weeks!

"Things are better now, but you will still have to pass a medical exam. Tonight is the beginning of the Sabbath, and we will not be able to buy your ticket until Monday. How much money do you have with you?"

"Thirty-three Deutsche marks."

"Good. A ticket to America costs around twenty-five marks for steerage. You should be fine. Now let us rest. My wife Lillian is preparing the Sabbath meal. We will walk to *shul* tomorrow."

At sundown, Lillian covered her head with lace and lit the two Sabbath candles while reciting the prayer:

בָּרוּךְ אַתָּה יְיָ אֱלֹהֵינוּ מֶלֶךְ הָעוֹלָם

Barukh atah Adonai, Eloheinu, melekh ha'olam
Blessed are Thou, O Lord, our God, King of the universe

אֲשֶׁר קִדְּשָׁנוּ בְּמִצְוֹתָיו וְצִוָּנוּ

asher kidishanu b'mitz'votav v'tzivanu
Who has sanctified us with His commandments and commanded us

לְהַדְלִיק נֵר שֶׁל שַׁבָּת: (אָמֵן)

l'had'lik neir shel Shabbat. (Amein)
to light the lights of Shabbat. (Amen)

That night, Arthur ate well with Moshe and his family. He was glad to rest before the next leg of his journey to America.

CHAPTER 4

The Gypsies Return
to Gav Gubernia

THE GYPSY CARAVAN MADE ITS way the last few kilometers back to the forest clearing surrounding Gav Gubernia. It was raining, and the roads were muddy. The wagon wheels got stuck in the potholes, and the horses had to pull hard to get them out. They had had a successful trip to Brody. The Gypsy men tended to some horses for their clients, and sold the yearlings for a good price. There were many music engagements in the nightclubs and bars. They even performed for the Mayor of Brody at his anniversary party. The women danced and told fortunes for many of the city women and men.

Durga was happy to be back. She couldn't wait to see Fanny and tell her the news of Arthur's escape from the soldiers. All the Gypsies welcomed them back. Some of the men were anxious to discuss several important issues with Django. They formed a circle with their wagons, unhitched the horses, and set up camp as much as possible. Then they went into the wagons to wait out the rain storm.

The rain lasted a couple of days. The Gypsies could only go out to perform the necessities of life, like cooking and tending to the animals. Finally, the rain let up. Durga mounted Manu and headed off to tell Fanny the news of her brother.

Fanny was helping Anna with spinning flax when Durga arrived and knocked on the door. "Come in," she said. "Did Arthur get to Brody? Tell us! Tell us!"

When Masha and the twins saw Durga, they came running in to hear the news. Durga related the story of how Arthur helped with chores on their way, and how he hid under the wagon in a hidden compartment when the soldiers stopped them at the border.

"He's all right," said Durga. "He got to Brody just fine, and we saw him at the bar that night with a gentleman. He seemed well taken care of. He must be in Hamburg by now, or even on the ship to America."

"Thank God," Masha said, breathing a sigh of relief as she turned to her daughters, "I can't wait to tell your father. Durga, we can't thank you and your parents enough for taking care of Arthur. Please do come for supper tonight with your brother and parents."

That night, Masha, Anna, and Fanny cooked a big meal of chicken soup, cheese biscuits with onion, cabbage rolls stuffed with meat, fresh baked bread, and noodle kugel, with mandelbrot for dessert. It was a worthy feast to honor Durga and her family, and to give thanks to God for Arthur's safe journey.

CHAPTER 5

Into the Wind on the Wings of a Prayer

ON MONDAY, MOSHE TOOK ARTHUR down to the steamship office to purchase a ticket to New York. He was able to get passage on the S.S. Hansa, which was sailing the following Friday at ten in the morning. But before Arthur could actually be guaranteed a space on the ocean liner, he had to face a medical exam by the German ship doctors. The appointment for the physical exam was set for Wednesday, and the ship was scheduled to sail two days later. He was a little nervous, as he had never before seen a doctor. Mama had her home remedies readily available for most childhood illnesses, such as drinking peppermint tea for a stomach ache, or taking rosehips and echinacea for colds, or applying to his chest a hot, sticky, smelly mustard plaster to relieve congestion. She recommended gargling with salt water for sore throats, and wrapping a knitted scarf around his neck at bedtime. Then there was the daily dose of cod liver oil for staying healthy. A store in town sold various herbal remedies, and for the most part they seemed to do the trick. But there were no medical doctors. The nearest one was some distance away in another town.

When Monday came, Moshe took Arthur down to the dock for his medical appointment. There, Arthur met up with hundreds of other men and women, hopeful passengers who were ordered to form two lines—men in one line and women in another. They were then ushered into two separate rooms and told to remove their clothes. At that point doctors examined them for skin disease, venereal disease, and tuberculosis. After checking heart and lungs with a stethoscope, they plucked an eyelash from each of them to check for trachoma, a highly contagious eye disease. If you had trachoma, it was certain you would not be allowed entry into the United States, and the steamship company would not allow you to board. Arthur was deeply humiliated by the exam. He had never had to undress in front of any strangers before. But he bore it, and he was lucky. He passed his medical exam and was approved to go on to America.

On Friday morning, Moshe took Arthur to the dock to board the S.S. Hansa, which was departing from Hamburg and bound for New York. Arthur was very excited. He had never been on a ship before. He walked proudly up the gangway and waved good-bye to Moshe.

"*Gay gazunta heit*, Go in health!" shouted Moshe.

Arthur took a place on the deck at the railing to wave good-bye. The whistle blew, and the ship set sail for America. Arthur's heart fluttered just a little as he watched the shoreline recede in the distance.

His excitement quickly dissipated as he realized how awful the conditions in steerage were. He was shown to a makeshift narrow room with two sets of bunks, three levels each, where he was placed in the middle bunk. There was so much noise and chaos as people were constantly moving about. Men and women were thrown together in the bunk rooms. The bathrooms were filthy, and a foul stench wafted in the air. There was no adequate place to bathe. People were soon lying seasick everywhere. The dining hall had six long wooden tables and primitive wooden benches to sit on. Everyone fought for a place at the table. Food was brought from the galley only twice a day and was served out of tin pails. It was barely palatable, and there was a shortage of good drinking water. Arthur yearned for his Mama's cheese biscuits now, as his thoughts turned to home.

After a couple of unbearable days, Arthur climbed the narrow, slippery steps to the second class deck, which was one floor above steerage. As he leaned over the railing to breathe some fresh air, he surveyed the endless sky, which was a brilliant blue. Large patches of white, fluffy clouds formed overhead. It reminded him of Mama's linen fibers before she spun them into thread.

Arthur contemplated the endless sky above him and the endless waves before him. He didn't know what lay ahead for him in America. What would it be like? Would he get a job? Would he find a place to live? Would he find Uncle Samuel? Would he meet friends he could talk with? All these thoughts were passing through his mind, when he became aware of a young man about his age standing next to him.

"*Shalom*, my name is Arthur Lusher. Do you speak Yiddish? What's your name?"

"My name is Hyman, Hyman Shaw," the young man replied in Yiddish.

"Where are you from? Are you traveling alone?"

"No," Hyman replied, "I'm traveling with my family, my Mama and Papa and my two sisters. We're from a Yiddish village in Belarus. We're going to America, where Papa can work and we can have a better life. Papa wants to start his own business and send us to school. Are you traveling alone?"

"Yes," Arthur replied sadly. "I leave behind my Mama and Papa, as well as four sisters and two brothers. The Cossacks were after Papa to force me into conscription, so they thought it best that I go to America to be safe. I have an Uncle Samuel there who lives in Cleveland, in the state of Ohio. I'm going to be staying with him."

"We're going to Cleveland too! Papa has a cousin who lives there. He's waiting for us to come."

Arthur and Hyman immediately became friends. They had much to talk about. They shared their hopes and fears. They related to each other their past experiences in Russia and their dreams for a new life in America.

For the rest of the trip, Arthur and Hyman were inseparable. Hyman introduced Arthur to his parents, Jacob and Bertha. They were glad to see that their son had found a friend.

The boys spent long hours on the deck together. Once, as they were looking out at the waves, they noticed a school of dolphins swimming alongside the ship, gracefully jumping in and out of the water. It looked as though they were playing with each other, seeing who could jump the farthest. The dolphins made squealing sounds as if they were talking to one another. Arthur felt they had a special message for him.

The nights were magical for him. The stars shone particularly bright against the dark night sky. Arthur could easily identify the many constellations, and he noticed the ship kept moving towards the Little Dipper. The waxing moon was like a bright mystical light whose rays formed a line of light that danced on the waves of the ocean. It was like a painting of light and dark. It was God's painting, God's way of showing his Glory and his Power.

During the long voyage, Arthur and Hyman talked about many things. One day the boys were on the deck, looking out into the vast ocean, and thinking about life in America. Both of them needed to leave their homes and the lives they were used to, and were forced to embrace this new way of life. They weren't even sure what it was yet. They started talking about what they missed back home. They also talked about their faith and what it meant to them.

Then Arthur asked Hyman, "Why don't you wear the *payot*, the side curls?"

Hyman explained, "I used to wear them. But as we were getting ready for our trip, Papa told me that wearing the side curls is more of a custom than a commandment. He said that there are many pious Jewish men who do not wear the *payot*. He had thought it best that we try to blend in with our new surroundings and not stand out, especially when we cross the border into America. We heard that most of the Jewish men in America do not wear side curls."

"I don't want to stand out," Arthur said. "I don't want the border guards to look at me with disdain. Will you help me cut them off?"

"Yes, if that's what you want," replied Hyman. "I will borrow a scissors from my mama."

As Hyman ran off to get the scissors, Arthur thought about this some more. Would the Rabbi approve? Would Papa approve? Would God approve? He wasn't sure about any of this, but he knew that he was his own man now and had to make decisions for himself based on his current circumstances. If Papa thought he'd be safer in America, then he should respect that and learn to embrace the customs of his new country. Arthur didn't want to jeopardize his safety in this new land, or to be made fun of, so he came to the conclusion that it would indeed be best for him to cut the *payot*.

Hyman returned with the scissors. "You do it, please," Arthur said, as he closed his eyes and turned his thoughts to God. He didn't want to disobey the Lord's commandments, but it seemed the right thing to do. "Let us say a prayer."

Together the boys sang: *"Baruch shem kavod mal-chuto l'olam va-ed*, Blessed is the Name of God's glorious kingdom, forever and ever." He wanted God to know that in no way did this act diminish his faith.

Arthur summoned his courage as Hyman cut the *payot*, first the right side, then the left. Hyman gave the curly brown locks to Arthur, who looked intently at his friend, as if to say with his eyes that what he had done was right. "To the success of our new life," he affirmed, "*Baruch atah Adonai Elohaynu Melech ha-olam,* Blessed art Thou, O Lord our God, King of the Universe." And with that prayer on his lips, Arthur released his curly locks into the wind, into the vast Universe in which God rules Supreme.

CHAPTER 6

The Seed of Creation

TWO WEEKS LATER, KALISARA SUMMONED the girls back for another lesson. With Nicola by her side, Fanny walked down the road to the Gypsy camp, where she met Durga by her wagon. Durga's long dark hair was tangled and draped over her shoulders. Her skirt was muddy, and her blouse was wrinkled. She had scratches on her arms. As Fanny approached, she smiled.

"Fanny," she said, "I just picked some black raspberries. Have some." She placed a painted clay bowl into Fanny's hands. Fanny took the bowl and grabbed some of the berries. They were tart and sweet and felt cool in her mouth, and she felt the coolness all the way down to the inside of her stomach.

"Thank you," Fanny replied gratefully.

"Let's go. Kalisara is waiting."

Nicola followed the girls as they walked around the camp to the back of the wagons. Kalisara was waiting for them, sitting on her chair under the generous shade of an oak tree. She wore a floral dress with a bright green scarf wrapped around her waist. The ends hung down in the front of her dress like the branches of a willow. An orange scarf was tied around her head. The edges fell down her back. She sat quietly. Her penetrating eyes seemed to be looking in and slightly up, but they were looking out. It was as if she was looking past the personalities of the girls and into their souls. She beckoned them to sit on the grass before her. As they sat down to listen, Nicola curled up beside Fanny and went to sleep.

Kalisara began. "In order to give a truthful reading for a client, first you must learn to sit still and become one with the truth. You must quell your wandering thoughts. You must become so silent that whatever comes up for you arises from the deepest, most peaceful part of your being. In this way, what you say comes not from what you think, but from an inner knowing, the part of you that automatically knows what comes next—the part that knows what the universe, in all its possibility, is presenting before you. It is like knowing how the dice land before they land. What you see is as clear as looking at your own hand.

"Think of the apple tree. In the winter there are only bare branches, with frost clinging to the bark. Even then, with the mind's eye you can see spring blossoms and sweet summer fruit. You see the leaves turn color in autumn and drop off the tree. All this you know without even looking at the tree, because this is the natural order.

"To attain this clarity you must learn to tap into the part of you that is completely still. To dwell in this state, sit quietly and listen to your breath. Start to pay attention to the space between breaths, the silent space where the breath subsides, and before it rises again. This is the seed of creation. From this internal space of tranquility, everything and anything can arise. In this world, everything must follow a natural order. These are the laws of nature, dictated by the elements that surround an individual. But in addition to natural law, know that there is also *divine intervention*. In this case something unexpected could occur, something out of the pattern of the predictable. And it is for this reason you need to look at the cards from the depth of your being—so that what you see is what you know, not what you think.

"Now let us sit silently for a few minutes to practice connecting with this inner space."

Fanny and Durga sat quietly at the feet of the old Gypsy Baba Kalisara, under the shade of the oak tree behind the Gypsy camp. Fanny followed her breath—first breathing in, then breathing out—until she lost track of it. After a while she didn't know whether she was breathing out or breathing in. There was only pure awareness.

CHAPTER 7

Ellis Island

AFTER TWO WEEKS, THE S.S. Hansa docked in New York. All the
passengers had to pass through Ellis Island, where their passports
would be inspected and stamped. The passengers, once again, had
to pass the medical exam. Arthur tried to stay close to Hyman and
his family. The Shaws had offered to accompany him to Cleveland.
Arthur was glad for that. They had made a plan to meet at the exit
gate in case they got separated. They all knew it was going to be a
grueling inspection that would take the whole day

The inspection was very frightening and intimidating for Arthur.
First the passengers were put into groups according to the ship's manifest, even before they got off the boat. Then, as they entered the
Customs and Immigration Building, they were kept in lines divided
by metal partitions. They were made to file past a doctor who was
looking for obvious maladies. If something was found that needed
further checking, a chalk mark was put onto that person's clothing.
Then they faced a series of questions from an examiner, to see if they
were of sound mind and body. Even the children were asked questions, to check if they were deaf or dumb.

Everyone was then shuffled into another area to be inspected by
a medical specialist in contagious disease. Men had to keep their
trousers open to be examined for venereal disease. The examiners

wore rubber gloves, but often did not bother to change them between examinations. This unnerved the new immigrants. These doctors continued to look for signs of tuberculosis, leprosy, or other skin or scalp disease. After that, they were shuffled forward to a third doctor, who plucked an eyelash to check for eye disease.

Finally, if they passed the medical exams, they were lined up according to nationality, whereby they were interrogated thoroughly by an Immigration officer. They were asked questions about their character and about their views on anarchism and crime. They were asked about their relatives, their work, and what had brought them to America. Did they have a job? How much money did they carry? Were they ever in prison? Could they read and write? Was anyone meeting them? Where were they going? The questions went on and on and on.

If they failed any of the exams or gave wrong answers to any of the questions, they could be detained at Ellis Island, sometimes for weeks—or, even worse, they could be sent back to Europe. Arthur was pretty worn out by the end of the day, but fortunately and gratefully he passed the Customs and Immigration inspection, and his passport was stamped for entry into the United States of America.

He waited outside the gate for Hyman and his family. After some time they all reunited. They were too exhausted to talk, and together they boarded the ferry to the southern tip of Manhattan Island, to an area in New York City known as "The Battery." From there they would try to find a hotel room. The following day, they would all board a train for Cleveland.

They were lucky to find a hotel near the ferry landing. They ate dinner, and after washing up they all fell fast asleep. The next morning, after a well-needed rest, Arthur and his new-found family woke up fresh and a little daunted at their new surroundings. They washed up, checked out of the hotel and ate breakfast at a nearby diner. They took a trolley to the train station. There they hoped to get tickets on a train bound for Cleveland. They were relieved to learn there was a passenger train leaving that afternoon for Cleveland and other destinations west. They would arrive the next day. Arthur thought he'd send a telegram to his Uncle Samuel, to inform him of his impending arrival. Luckily, there was a telegraph office in the train station.

Arthur was amazed at how large New York City was. It had tall buildings and wide streets with gas lamps that were lit up at night. There were many horseless carriages being driven among the horse-drawn carriages. It was a magnificent city in the midst of change. It was 1899. There was a beautiful public park called Central Park, where autumn leaves displayed their bright colors. Arthur noticed many finely dressed men and women strolling on the sidewalks and children playing in the streets. It was a lively city, full of shops and stores of every kind. Arthur stared in awe at everything he saw. This was indeed a new world, but one which he was quite certain he would come to love.

CHAPTER 8

The Gypsies Prepare to Leave Gav Gubernia

AUTUMN SET IN. SHE CAME in all her glorious colors: reds, oranges, and golden yellows. Days started to get shorter. The Gypsies were packing their wagons, and preparing to move on to their winter homes near the city of Odessa. The winters were too long and too harsh for them to remain in their wagons. They had cabins to go to just outside the city, where they could keep warm and endure the long winter nights. The Gypsy women would then continue to tell fortunes in the city, and the men would continue to play music in the bars and nightclubs. Life would go on.

Under the bright red-and-orange canopy of the forest, Fanny, Durga, and Nicola were out in the woods picking mushrooms together. Fanny was feeling sad to see Durga leave and their sessions with Kalisara come to an end.

"Will you be back?" Fanny asked.

"I don't know," answered Durga. "That depends on what Django and the elders decide."

Nicola was busy sniffing some droppings from a squirrel. Then she lifted her head, with her ears standing straight up as she listened intently to a distant sound. She sniffed the air. When she seemed

55

content that she was able to identify the mysterious noise, she put her nose back down on the ground and continued to sniff the plants, the bugs, and the earth.

"I want you to have this scarf I knitted for you," said Fanny, as she reached into her shoulder bag. "It's something to remember me by."

"I shall always think of you," Durga replied, looking directly at Fanny. "And in the future, before I read the cards I will remember you in my moment of quiet."

"In that moment I will remember you too, Durga. In that way we will always be together."

The girls hugged and parted. "Come on, Nicola. Let's go home."

Fanny walked home wistfully, with Nicola by her side. While slowly putting one foot in front of the other, she thought about Durga and Kalisara. She admired the inner beauty and generosity of Durga, and she wanted to be like that. Then she reflected on the mysterious Kalisara, a kind, strong woman of wisdom who seemed to embody the very power of nature. Fanny wanted to be like that. From her family she learned the struggle for survival. But from the Gypsies she learned the wisdom that surpasses all struggle. She came to know of a gentle yielding to the powers that hold sway over our lives. She learned that we can be prepared to engage in a graceful and dignified manner with whatever comes our way

CHAPTER 9

Anna's Wedding

WITH AUTUMN ALSO CAME THE excitement of Anna's marriage to Martin, the tailor's son. Mama and Papa had arranged with Martin's parents for the wedding to take place in October. Anna spent all of September sewing her wedding dress. Fanny helped with sewing on the decorative beads and lace. Masha was busy making dresses for Lilly and Lana, who were so excited because they were going to be the flower girls.

Martin was a very skilled tailor, for he had learned from his father. He was a professional in designing clothing as well as in his knowledge of textiles. He knew about the different types of thread, what kinds of cloth to use, and how to make patterns. Furthermore, he could make hats. Jewish men always wore long black coats and black hats in the Synagogue. Anna was a good seamstress too, and was particularly skillful at finishing work. She could knit scarves, gloves, and hats. All of her skills would be a benefit to the family business.

Anna and Martin had known each other for a long time, having grown up together in the *shtetl*. They were quite fond of each other. It was a good match.

Temple Beth El was a simple wooden building located in the town square. It was the center of life in the community of the people of Gav Gubernia. All holy days and rites of passage were celebrated in the Synagogue. In the main sanctuary there was a commanding ark, where the Torah scroll was housed behind two wooden doors and a curtain. The Star of David was painted in gold on the front of each door. There were rooms at the back for study, and a small kitchen where food could be prepared for holy days and special occasions. There was a balcony, where the women sat during the services. Reb Zalman had been the head Rebbe for many years. He had seen both Martin and Anna grow up. He had performed Martin's *brit milah*, the circumcision admitting the new male child into the covenant of God. He had presided over the marriage of Masha and Abe, as well as the marriage of Martin's parents. He knew the families well. He was also pleased with the match.

On the Sabbath night before the marriage was to take place, Martin was called to read from the Torah in the Synagogue. Anna couldn't be present, because the bride and groom were not allowed to see each other for seven days prior to the wedding. On the morning of the wedding, Anna went to the *mikvah* to immerse herself in the ritual bath. This was to signify her purity and readiness for married life. As she sat in the waters of the *mikvah,* she reflected on the new life she was about to embark upon. She was a little anxious, but glad.

Young girls grew up knowing that one day their parents would choose a husband for them. All their lives they waited in nervous anticipation and excitement for that day to come. Anna knew marriage came with new duties and responsibilities, first to her husband and then to their children. In the *mikvah* she prayed to God, vowing that she was ready to take up this new life with Martin and that she would hold dear in her heart all the sacred laws.

After leaving the *mikvah,* Anna went home to prepare herself. She was fasting today until after the wedding. The wedding day is considered a most holy and sacred day for the bride and groom. It is considered a personal *Yom Kippur,* a personal day of atonement. It is a day when all the past mistakes of the couple are forgiven by God. With the wedding vows, the two souls merge together and become one soul. This "new soul" is seen as pure.

The morning of the wedding, colorful autumn leaves blew in front of the Synagogue and lay strewn on the steps, as if they were God's offerings to the bride and groom. Before the wedding ceremony, Anna sat in one of the back rooms of the Synagogue, where she received her guests. Martin received his guests in the sanctuary, as the two were forbidden to see each other. Then Martin's mother and Anna's mother stood together and broke a plate. "This union is a serious commitment," Masha spoke. "Just as a plate can never be fully repaired, neither can a broken relationship. We offer blessings on the couple, that they may lead a happy and fulfilling life."

It was time for Martin to veil his bride. Accompanied by his family and friends, he went to the room where Anna was sitting. Anna smiled at Martin when she saw him come into the room. Then she quickly looked down in modesty. Martin's heart fluttered as he ceremoniously took the veil of Anna's crown from behind her head and placed it over her face. He felt the softness of the lace, and in that gesture he vowed to protect his wife always.

The wedding ceremony was now ready to begin. The sacred canopy, the *chuppah,* was in place, adorned with pine boughs and ribbons. The couple would stand beside one another under this symbol of the home they would make together. It was open on all sides, to remind them to welcome all guests into their home with unconditional hospitality. First, Martin's parents escorted him down the aisle. Next, Martin's and Anna's brothers and sisters walked slowly down the aisle. Then came the twins, Lilly and Lana, in their pretty pink dresses, carrying baskets of flower petals. With great care they threw the petals down on the path their big sister Anna would soon walk upon. They were excited, and could hardly restrain themselves from giggling.

Next Anna came, accompanied by Masha and Abe. Anna's heart was pounding with excitement. She tried to concentrate on her breathing, so as to keep it steady. Martin was waiting for her at the front of the *chuppah*. There, Masha and Abe handed Anna to Martin. He took her arm to escort her to the podium, where Reb Zalman was waiting. As he held his bride close, Martin felt a tingling sensation in his body. When they got to the front of the *chuppah*, Anna looked down in modesty and smiled as she slowly walked around Martin seven times. This was to symbolize the new life they were building together, and to seal the vow of the seven blessings.

Reb Zalman was dressed in his long black coat. His curly gray hair stuck out on the sides of his black yarmulke. He had a full gray beard, and his kind eyes were magnified behind the lenses of his eyeglasses. He looked at Anna and Martin with love and pride, as if they were his own children. With his gracious glance upon the couple, he bestowed his blessing for the union. And with great love, he began to speak the sacred words:

Blessed art Thou, O Lord, our God, King of the universe, who has created the fruit of the vine.

. . . who created everything for His Glory.

. . . who creates man.

. . . who creates man in His image, perpetuating life.

. . . who gladdens Zion with her children.

. . . who grants perfect joy to these loving companions.

Blessed art Thou, O Lord, who causes the groom to rejoice with his bride.

And with these seven blessings, Martin and Anna were united as man and wife.

As Martin listened to the liturgy and said his marriage vows, he seemed a little taller, a little more responsible. He became a man in front of the eyes of everyone who was assembled there. When it came time for the bride and groom to sip wine from the same glass, he drank first. And then, with careful attention and with a feeling of protection and love, he offered a sip to Anna. And when he stepped on the glass to break it and seal the marriage, he did so with gusto.

Thus the joyous occasion of the marriage of Martin and Anna took place, and Anna left her mama's house to live with her husband and start their own family.

CHAPTER 10

A Letter from Arthur

WITH ANNA GONE, MORE RESPONSIBILITIES of the household fell to
Fanny. She had to prepare food and help cook, as well as take care of
the boys and the twins. Lilly and Lana were old enough now to participate in doing some of the chores. They could help with sweeping
and dusting the house, with bringing wood in for the fire, and with
preparing meals. Slowly, Fanny found more jobs they could do.

That winter, Fanny watched the first snowfall from her window.
The snowflakes filled the sky, gently floating down, and the brown
earth slowly turned to white. She watched as icicles began to form
on the eaves of the roof, where they hung down to the tops of the
windows. As the winter wore on, the boys had to shovel the walkway
and help with feeding the chickens, milking the cow, and tending the
horses. They also had to work with Papa in his shoemaking shop.
They were learning how to tan hides and prepare them to craft them
into shoes. They also learned how to make the soles, and how to sew
them together.

That winter, Anna was with child. Masha and Abe were delighted. Fanny's thoughts turned to Durga and Kalisara. Where were
they now? Fanny imagined they were safe and warm in their cabins.
Then her thoughts turned to Arthur. She wondered what life was like
in America. Did Arthur like it? Did he make friends?

Arthur had written a long letter to Mama and Papa. He had arrived in New York and had made it past Immigration. With the help of the family he had met on the steamship, the Shaws, he was escorted to Cleveland, where he had met up with Uncle Samuel. He settled in and got a job working in a steel factory, making pails and stove parts. Soon he was able to rent a room of his own in a boarding house near the factory. He worked hard, ten hours a day and six days a week. Arthur missed his family terribly. And he was working so hard, he didn't have time to cook or to keep his room clean or wash his clothes. He sent his love to all.

The New Year came. It was now 1900, the start of a new century. Everyone wondered what this new Twentieth Century would bring. They prayed to God that the pogroms would end this year. Papa and the boys continued to sell shoes in the marketplace, and Masha continued to make linen.

Then, one spring day, a letter from Arthur arrived. He was doing well, and he was spending each Sabbath at the Shaw home. His friend Hyman got a job working for a house painter. Hyman was learning about the different types of brushes and paints and about how to choose colors. Everyone was able to find work. But Arthur felt very lonely without his family. He was still working long, tiring hours, and was thus feeling a bit down. He wrote to Mama and Papa, requesting that they please send Fanny to America to keep him company and to help with the household chores. He wanted her to travel second class so she wouldn't have to bear the indignities of steerage. He planned to send the money for Fanny's passage, and thought he would have enough saved in a year's time.

Masha and Abe thought long and hard about Arthur's proposal. They thought about Fanny's future in the *shtetl*. At best, Fanny would marry someone who would be forever impoverished. At best, Fanny's sons would have to figure out a way to avoid conscription or else leave home. In America there would be a chance that Fanny could marry and her children could lead a better life. They could go to school and lift themselves out of poverty. It was a worthy opportunity to consider.

Masha and Abe discussed the proposal with Fanny. They asked her if she wanted to go to America. Fanny didn't have to think too much about it. She was excited at the prospect of leaving the predictable life of the *shtetl*, which led nowhere, for something unknown and possibly grand. She was curious about the ways of America, and was excited to think about meeting all kinds of different people from around the world. She was also excited to think about crossing the ocean in second class! She had never gone beyond Gav Gubernia. She wanted to see and taste what the world was like—and thus felt more than ready for this adventure.

"Yes," answered Fanny. "I do want to go to America. I am looking forward to having new experiences and seeing what the world is like beyond Gav Gubernia. I do miss Arthur, and I wouldn't be alone. I would be with him, and would be a help to him. Please do let me go."

It was hard for Masha and Abe to say yes. First, Arthur had left home, then Anna, and now Fanny would be leaving. But they realized it would be best for Fanny, and so they consented.

"We will write Arthur and tell him to start making preparations," Papa said.

Fanny was beside herself in anticipation. She could hardly wait for the day to arrive. That spring, the Gypsies did not return to Gav Gubernia. Fanny was greatly disappointed. She was hoping her friend Durga would return, and she was hoping to learn more from Kalisara. But Kalisara had made it clear to Fanny, the last time they met, that she had already learned what needed to be learned. Fanny just needed to practice.

She practiced first on the boys at home. It gave her a little confidence. Next she read cards for Anna. Her confidence soon grew, when other wives in the community started coming to her for advice from the cards. It helped that Fanny focused on her breath and thought of Durga before she began each reading, just as they had promised each other. As she interpreted the cards, she felt Kalisara's inner guidance—it was almost as if Kalisara was speaking *through* her.

CHAPTER 11

The Magic of Tea Leaves

FANNY'S FASCINATION TO LEARN ABOUT the hidden mysteries in order to help others was continuing to grow, and one summer day she went to visit Mrs. Rosenthal.

"I'm going to pay a visit to Mrs. Rosenthal," Fanny told Mama.

"Fanny, make sure you take some challah to give her. Tell her *shalom* for me," Mama said, "and be back by supper."

Fanny grabbed her shawl and ran out of the house, carrying the challah in her shoulder bag. Nicola followed her down the road, wagging her tail in anticipation of a new adventure. As they walked through town, Nicola spotted a bunny rabbit. While barking she began to chase after it. The bunny leaped in the air and scampered under a nearby thick bush to safety. Nicola ran after it, whining all the way. She proceeded to sniff and scratch at the bottom of the bush. When she felt certain she couldn't get to the bunny, she cocked her head and gave up the chase, returning to Fanny's side.

When Fanny got to Mrs. Rosenthal's house, she knocked on the door.

"Welcome. Come in," Mrs. Rosenthal answered the door with a big smile.

"Thank you," Fanny replied. "Here's a challah Mama sent." After offering the bread to her neighbor, she told Nicola to wait outside.

Mrs. Rosenthal lived in Gav Gubernia. She was in her early fifties. All her children had grown up and were married off, although she had nine grandchildren who visited often. As the town counselor, she was also often visited by neighbors who sought her advice and solutions to personal problems. These ranged from marital discord and matchmaking advice to problems with depression or grief. She would help them by reading tea leaves or reading patterns from molten lead. Sometimes she devised other solutions to help, by instilling power into ordinary objects such as coins or chickens' eggs. Someone else might seek her help in interpreting a dream. She was a storehouse of folk knowledge and cures. Today Fanny was visiting to learn tea leaf reading.

"Sit down, Fanny. We'll talk while I boil the water for tea." Mrs. Rosenthal offered Fanny a chair at the kitchen table. She poured fresh water into the cast iron kettle and set it on the stove.

"It is important to create a sense of ritual and space for the client. Boil the water while they are in the kitchen with you. Set aside a special cup for tea leaf reading. It should have a clear white bottom.

"The size of the tea leaf is important. If the leaves are too big, they will tend to clump together in one area. Choose a tea leaf that is medium in size, so the patterns they create are diverse.

"Begin a friendly conversation with your neighbor to gently find out what the problem is that brings them to you. Be informal. Make your neighbor feel at ease. Often when someone has a problem they are tense and may have shoulder aches, headaches, or other bodily aches. By making them feel comfortable and safe enough to talk about their problem, the body also relaxes. Ask them to focus on their breath three times. Once they are relaxed in body and mind, a space is created for the answer to come.

"Now the water has boiled."

Mrs. Rosenthal asked Fanny to put a pinch of tea leaves in the cup, which she filled with boiling water. The leaves scattered about in the water. Most settled to the bottom, but some of the lighter ones floated on the top.

"Fanny, let the tea steep, and then drink the tea. Don't drink all of it. Let a small amount of water remain." Slowly, Fanny began to drink the tea. She felt as if this was a special moment, and she wanted to savor it. Mrs. Rosenthal enjoyed a cup of tea as well, and they continued to talk. She asked about her mama and papa and the children, and about Anna and Martin. She knew Anna was with child. As Fanny answered, she noticed her mind relaxed, and she was less focused on herself. Before she knew it, there was only a small amount of water left at the bottom of the cup.

"Good," Mrs. Rosenthal continued. "Now take three deep breaths and swirl the water in the cup three times." Fanny closed her eyes, listening to the air as she breathed. She noticed that the air made a sound as she breathed in, and it made a different sound as she breathed out. She felt her lungs expand and contract as the air filled them and then left.

Fanny opened her eyes and began to swirl the water in the cup three times.

"As you swirl the cup, slowly pour out the remaining water into the saucer," Mrs. Rosenthal instructed.

Fanny poured out the remaining water. Left at the bottom of the cup were clumps of tea leaves.

"Now point the handle towards the questioner. Read the leaves clockwise, starting from the handle. Leaves to the right of the handle indicate the future. Leaves to the left indicate the past. The further the leaves are from the handle, the further away the events are, either in time or in physical space.

"First look to see if any patterns or signs jump out at you. Any drops left in the cup indicate tears. These can be tears of joy, or of sorrow. A large clump of tea leaves indicates trouble. If they are near the handle, it is trouble caused by your own making. If they are away from the handle, it is trouble that is not your fault.

"Tea leaves on the *rim* of the cup represent recent events. Tea leaves lying at the *bottom* represent more distant events. Tea-stalks indicate people: long stalks, men, and shorter stalks, women. Slanted stalks are untrustworthy people. You can read the patterns formed by the groups of tea leaves—and to form a complete picture, you can read the patterns formed in between the tea leaves on the inside of the cup."

Fanny peered into her tea cup, wondering what it all meant. There were a lot of leaves to the right of the handle, and very few to the left. There was one stray leaf on the rim of the cup. "Your future is bright, Fanny," Mrs. Rosenthal said. "There is very little of the past left for you here. There is, however, one incident that will carry you into your future, and your future will unfold in a distant place."

Fanny saw the sun moving towards the horizon. "I must go home now to help with supper. Thank you for the instruction. May I return to watch as you read the leaves for a client?"

"Yes, certainly. Come this Thursday afternoon at two o'clock. I am expecting Mrs. Levin. Until then, *shalom.*"

Fanny left the house. Nicola was curled up on the porch, sleeping, waiting for Fanny. "Come on, Nicola. Let's go home."

Fanny and Nicola walked down the road. A bunny rabbit darted quickly in front of them, but Nicola was too sleepy to care.

CHAPTER 12

On the Way to America

FANNY RETURNED SEVERAL TIMES THAT summer to Mrs. Rosenthal's house, where she learned the technique of reading tea leaves. Soon she started to read tea leaves for the boys at home, and then for Anna.

That summer, a baby girl was born to Anna and Martin. She was a beautiful child, with soft red hair and light blue eyes. Anna named her Rachel. Mama and Papa were thrilled, as Rachel was their first grandchild. Mama was now quite busy helping Anna care for her. On the Sabbath after Rachel was born, Martin was called to the Synagogue to read from the Torah. Two weeks later, Mama invited Reb Zalman and all the neighbors to the house for a special blessing for Rachel and Anna. It was a celebration to welcome the new baby into the community. Fanny and the girls helped Mama cook for the gathering. They prepared challah, cheese blintzes, and noodle kugel.

When Rachel turned one year old and was just taking her first steps, Mama and Papa received a letter from Arthur containing the money to buy passage for Fanny to join him in America. Fanny was ready and determined. Mama and Papa had contacted Moshe in Hamburg, asking again for his assistance in helping Fanny obtain passage on an ocean liner to New York.

In preparation for her journey, Papa took Fanny to the District Office to get her passport stamped with an exit permit. The Russian police were glad to get rid of another Jew, and they stamped it with no qualms and with no questions asked.

On the next full moon, Fanny would depart for America. Papa traded some shoes at the market place for a new steamer trunk for Fanny. It was quite large, and she could fit many things into it. It had hard sides and a place for a lock in front, from where it opened up like a treasure chest. From the locksmith, Papa bought a new metal padlock and shiny key. He gave it to Fanny so she could lock her trunk.

Fanny spent many days thinking about what to take. She was pleased that she could take all her clothes and most of her belongings. She had a special deck of hand-painted cards that Kalisara had given her, and a beautiful porcelain tea cup and saucer that Mrs. Rosenthal had given her to use for tea leaf reading. She would certainly take these and would treasure them as gifts from her teachers. Mama had sewn a new suit for her to wear when she got to America. It was a long skirt with blue vertical stripes, with a matching jacket and a blue hat. To wear under it, Fanny took a white blouse that buttoned up to her neck. Samuel made her a new pair of black leather shoes that laced all the way up. Anna knitted a matching hat, scarf, and gloves. Lilly and Lana gave her a drawing of a house with Nicola and all the children playing in front.

Mama cooked for two days before Fanny's departure. She was worried Fanny would go hungry on her journey. She made jerky and baked cheese biscuits, onion bagels, and mandelbrot. She gave her some apples to take as well. She also gave her two brass candlesticks for celebrating the Sabbath.

Fanny went to say good-bye to Anna, Martin, and Rachel. She picked up Rachel and squeezed her tight. "Good-bye, Rache-la, I'll miss you."

Then she visited Mrs. Rosenthal, to thank her for imparting the knowledge of tea leaf reading and other folk wisdom to her. "*Gay gazentah heit*, Go in health," Mrs. Rosenthal told her.

She went to the Synagogue for a blessing from Reb Zalman. "Another child going to America," he mused. "It is a sad day for Gav Gubernia. You take my blessings with you."

Fanny felt sad to say good-bye to her friends and family, but she was also ready to embark on a new adventure.

On the morning of her departure, Mama, Papa, Samuel, Joseph, the twins, and Nicola all accompanied her to the train station in Odessa. They all hugged and kissed as they waited for the train to arrive on the platform. The girls were sad.

"We'll miss you," they said, and gave Fanny a big hug.

The boys hugged Fanny, too. Mama cried. Papa uttered a big sigh.

"Remember," said Papa, "Arthur wants you to travel *second class*. You have the money he sent. Moshe will meet you at the train station in Hamburg."

Nicola jumped up onto Fanny's leg and whimpered. Fanny patted Nicola, "Good-bye, dear friend. The girls will take care of you now."

They heard the whistle of the train in the distance, after which it pulled into the station. The porter helped Fanny with her steamer trunk. Taking in a deep breath, she boarded the train. She walked up each step consciously and with determination, and she quickly found a seat. This was the first time Fanny had ever been on a train. When she looked out the window at her family, tears fell down her cheeks. She knew she would never again see them, who meant everything to her. After a few minutes the engineer blew the whistle.

As the train pulled out of the station, Fanny sat quietly for a while, breathing in and feeling the love of her family and community. As she closed her eyes, she could see the apple trees and the forest. She could see Mama and Papa, and her sisters and brothers. She could see the Gypsy camp, and Durga and Kalisara. She saw it all in her mind's eye.

Then she breathed out and opened her eyes to look out the train window. She was in new terrain that she had never seen before. All of her senses were on alert. She began to look at the city, noticing the big buildings and the paved streets. There were men at work, women shopping, and children playing. Soon the train left the city and was traveling through the countryside. They passed by orchards and fields, where peasants, dressed in burlap trousers, black boots, and large brimmed hats, were hard at work. Fanny noticed sheep and horses among the herds of cows in the fields. She loved the countryside.

After several hours, they stopped at the border. Russian soldiers got on the train to check passports. They approached each passenger very brusquely, asking to see their papers. When a soldier came up to Fanny, she showed him her stamped passport.

"Where are you going?" he asked.

"To America," replied Fanny. The soldier laughed at her cynically and gave her passport back to her.

Soon the train arrived in Brody and stopped there for a long time. Some passengers got off, while others boarded the train. She was now in Austria-Hungary. It felt to her like she was in a new country. Everything looked and smelled different than at home, and the people seemed a little more relaxed.

Fanny noticed a lot of Jewish passengers boarding the train at Brody. There were young men in yarmulkes, women carrying children on their hips, and some families. Many of the children were crying, as their environment was rapidly changing.

Fanny was hungry. She was grateful that Mama had prepared some food for her. Unpacking the kerchief, she found cheese biscuits and jerky, which she ate with relish. Then she munched on an apple and drank some water, feeling Mama's love in every bite.

"All aboard!" she heard the cries from the station platform. The porters were shouting through a large megaphone in three languages: German, Hungarian, and Russian. As the train pulled out of the station, Fanny was feeling full and sat back in her seat. Mesmerized by the motion of the train, she dozed off peacefully.

"Hamburg, next stop. Hamburg, next stop," shouted the porter as he came through the car. Fanny opened her eyes and shook herself awake. She stepped off the train when it came to a stop, and waited on the platform for the porter to bring her steamer trunk. She thanked him and gave him a few coins. Standing on the platform, she straightened up her shoulders as she became aware of a new sense of self-confidence and self-suffiency within herself that she hadn't noticed before. She felt taller and more mature.

"*Shalom aleichem*. Excuse me, are you Fanny Lusher?" a voice asked in Yiddish.

"*Aleichem shalom*. Yes I am," Fanny turned around. "Are you Moshe?"

"Yes, yes. Let me help you with your luggage."

Moshe picked up the steamer trunk and escorted Fanny outside the station, where Moshe's wife was waiting in the carriage.

"*Shalom*, Fanny. I am Lillian, Moshe's wife. Come sit beside me, and we will take you home."

Fanny was so glad to be taken care of. At Moshe's house Lillian had prepared a lovely dinner in honor of Fanny's arrival. The children had carefully set the table with their best porcelain china. Moshe, Lillian, and their three children all sat down together with Fanny, and after the blessing, they began to eat. During dinner, Moshe and Lillian told Fanny about Arthur's visit with them and asked how he was doing.

"He's doing very well," replied Fanny. "He is working on an assembly line in a metal parts factory. He works so hard, he asked if I could come to America to keep him company. I am excited to go to America. He saved up and sent enough money so that I can travel second class! After his experience on the ship in third class, he vowed not to make me endure the rough and unsanitary conditions of steerage."

"Very well, Fanny. That's good," Moshe replied. "We've also heard many stories about the bad conditions of steerage. So many people get sick. There is not enough food and water, and nowhere to clean up. I am glad for you. Tomorrow we will go to purchase your ticket for New York. At the dock you will have to take a medical exam as well."

"Oh," exclaimed Fanny. "When does that take place?"

"When we buy your ticket the agent will assign you a time before sailing," Moshe explained.

"What do you plan to do in America, Fanny?" asked Lillian.

"I can do many things," Fanny said proudly. "I can cook and sew. I am good with numbers. And I read playing cards and tea leaves."

"How fascinating," Lilian responded. "Can you read *my* tea leaves?"

"Certainly," Fanny said with confidence. "I learned from Mrs. Rosenthal in our town. Do you have a tea cup that has a clear bottom?"

"Yes, I believe so." Lillian started to rummage through her cupboards. "Yes, here's one."

"Good. Start to boil water for some tea. Then pour the tea for us in each cup."

Lillian boiled the water and poured tea for Fanny, Moshe, and herself. Lillian told her children they could go to their rooms and play, but they were far more interested in the tea leaf reading, and so they stayed in the dining room to watch. Fanny told Lillian to drink most of the tea, but to save a little water at the bottom of the cup. Then she instructed her to take three deep breaths, and then to swirl the tea leaves in the cup three times and pour out the remaining liquid. Fanny sat across from Lillian and positioned the handle of the tea cup towards her.

Fanny steadied her breath and then looked into the tea cup. It wasn't like looking directly *into* the tea cup. It was more like looking *beyond* the tea leaves in the cup. Her vision relaxed, and she could see patterns begin to form in and around the leaves.

Fanny began to speak: "Lillian, you are a very kind-hearted person who will live a long life. Your children will be successful. In the future, some trouble will occur. Though not of your own doing, it will force you to travel a long distance from your home. But you will be safe, and everything will come out all right in the end."

Lillian was astonished. The children looked at each other in amazement. They had never seen this before. Everyone sat quiet for a while. Then Lillian spoke, "Children, it's time for bed."

The children moaned and protested that they wanted to stay up with Fanny, but with the urging of their parents they marched off to prepare for bed.

The next day, Moshe took Fanny to the dock, to help her purchase a second class ticket. The next steamship sailing for New York, the S.S. Nordan, was leaving in five days. Second class meant that she was one deck up from steerage. She would be sharing a small cabin with another passenger, and there would be a shared bathroom nearby. There were no portholes, but she could step outside her cabin and sit on the deck chairs or simply walk around. Fanny felt proud she could travel second class. The agent at the steamship ticket office asked her to come back in two days for a medical exam.

On the day of the checkup, she didn't know what to expect. She wasn't used to seeing a doctor. She was only used to Mama's home remedies, like gargling with salt water, applying mustard plasters on her chest, drinking tea, and keeping her neck warm with a woolen scarf. There were a lot of people who had come for the medical exam. Fanny was led into a room, where a nurse looked at her body to see if there was any skin or scalp disease. One doctor checked her heart and lungs with a stethoscope, while another doctor plucked an eyelash to check for trachoma.

Fanny passed her medical exam, and she was cleared to board the S.S. Nordan when it sailed in three days. The rest of the time, Fanny helped Lillian with the household chores and with the children, who had grown very fond of her.

The day of departure came. Fanny washed her hair and bathed. She put on a clean skirt and blouse, pinned her hair in a bun on the top of her head, and repacked her steamer trunk. She also carried a shoulder bag. Lillian had given her some bagels, cheese, fruit, and jerky to take with her on her journey. Fanny was glad for that. Lillian and Moshe accompanied her to the dock, to see her off.

"Thank you so much for everything," Fanny said with heartfelt gratitude. "I couldn't have gotten this far without you."

"*Gay gazenta heit*, Go in health," shouted Lillian, as Fanny walked up the boarding platform. "Remember to write to us when you get to America."

"Blessings on your way," shouted Moshe. "May you have a good life in America."

Fanny paid attention to each step she took as she boarded the ship. Finally on her way to America, she felt the impact of this new leg of her journey. She was proud and dazed at the same time, and wished Mama and Papa could see her now.

She found her second class cabin on the lower deck, in room 609, where the porter had placed her steamer trunk. Then she went to the railing of the deck to look for Moshe and Lillian. She saw them in the crowd and waved to them. The Captain of the S.S. Nordan rang its loud and booming bell three times, signaling it was about to depart. Fanny took in a deep breath of the fresh ocean air and closed her eyes. Her heart fluttered. She had never been on a ship before. Feeling a little dizzy as the ship pulled out of the harbor, she held onto the rail, and after a few minutes she got used to the movement. She watched the skyline of the Hamburg harbor as they slowly pulled away, until it was out of sight.

Good-bye, homeland, she thought. *You nurtured me and brought me to this point in life. I thank you for your gifts. I thank Mama and Papa for teaching me faith and how to live in the world.* Tears dropped down her cheeks as she thought of Mama and Papa and all that they had sacrificed. She knew she would never see them again.

Once the ship was out in the open ocean, Fanny decided to unpack a few things, so she returned to her cabin. Upon opening the door, she found her cabin mates were already settling in.

"*Shalom aleichem,*" Fanny said. "I am Fanny Lusher, and I am going to live with my brother, whose home is in Cleveland, Ohio."

"*Aleichem shalom,*" greeted the woman with a big smile. "I am Malci Adler, and these are my two children. My son Herman is six and my daughter Rachel is three. We are from Rumania, and we are traveling to join my husband Sol in Brooklyn, New York."

Malci was a young orthodox Jewish wife and mother, who covered her hair with a wig. Fanny noticed that she was very beautiful.

"Oh. I have a young niece named Rachel, whom I miss very much. We'll have a good time," Fanny said, as she squeezed Rachel's little hand.

Right away the two women became good friends. There were two bunks in the cabin. The children shared a lower bunk, and Malci slept next to them. Fanny slept on the top of the other bunk. They both used the extra top bunk to place their things.

As they were unpacking, Malci asked, "Are you married?"

"No."

She went on. "My husband Sol and I were married seven years ago. We lived in Siebenbürgen. He left for America three years ago. He hasn't even seen Rachel. He's worked very hard to earn enough money to send for us. He settled in Brooklyn, where our cousins live. Brooklyn has a large Jewish community with five Synagogues!"

"I come from Gav Gubernia, near Odessa."

As Fanny unpacked her steamer trunk, Malci noticed Fanny's deck of cards that Kalisara had given her.

"Do you read cards?" asked Malci.

"Yes, I learned from the Gypsies who lived outside our town."

"Would you read *my* fortune?"

"Yes, of course. We can do it tomorrow."

The rest of the day, Fanny got used to being on the ship. All the cabins shared a bathroom down the corridor. There was a woman's bathroom with a makeshift shower, several toilets, and a few sinks for washing up. Fanny was grateful for that. She noticed there were some chairs on the deck, and there was a larger room with tables and chairs where passengers could sit and talk or play cards and board games. Next to the sitting room, there was a dining hall where meals were served twice a day.

At six o'clock, Fanny, Malci, and the children went for dinner. They were joined by many passengers from second class. Fanny was excited to be around so many people from all over Europe. Thankfully, most were Jewish and so she could communicate in Yiddish no matter what country they came from. There were people from Germany, Poland, Rumania, Hungary, and Russia. There were also people from Lithuania and Latvia. They were all going to America to seek a better life. That night, Fanny made a lot of new friends.

The next day, Fanny read the cards for Malci in the large common room, where there were tables and chairs. Malci sat opposite Fanny. The kids hung onto the edge of the table and peered over to see. Standing on her tiptoes and staying close to her mama, Rachel watched with curiosity.

Fanny sat quietly for a moment, remembering Durga and Kalisara. She focused on her breath, and then laid out the Wagon Wheel spread. As she began the reading, other passengers gathered around, fascinated with what was going on. The reading was thorough, and it lasted for some time. At the end of it Malci was reassured of her and her children's future in America.

Some of the other passengers, who were watching with interest, asked Fanny if she could read their cards too. And so Fanny passed her time on the ship, reading the fortunes of the immigrants. Word drifted to the first class passengers, and soon Fanny was requested to go to first class to read fortunes there. Some of the passengers offered to pay her. She accepted whatever donations they offered. And in this way she was able to earn enough money to buy her train ticket to Cleveland.

One day, Fanny met Franz—a German man who spoke English. "Can you teach me to speak some English?" Fanny asked.

"I will trade you English lessons for a card reading," he replied.

Fanny agreed, and they met on the deck every day at two o'clock. She was glad to learn some basic English sentences, like how to request a train ticket, find out where the bathroom is, ask for directions, and so forth. As she learned more English, she grew more confident that when she arrived in America she could get by, maybe even enough to get her to Cleveland.

Like this, the days on the ship went by. Fanny played with the children and told them stories, read cards for passengers, and learned

English. She met many people and became well known on the ship as "The Fortune Teller."

Fanny loved the feel and the smell of the ocean breeze. She loved the expansive sky. One afternoon, she was looking over the ship railing, and to her wonder she saw a whale spouting and breaching in the distance. It was a glorious sight. She wondered for a moment about a whale's life in the ocean. *Whales are such majestic animals,* she thought. Then she noticed a school of bottleneck dolphins swimming near the ship, playfully jumping out of and into the water, making squealing noises to each other. Fanny was charmed by their playfulness. Then she looked up at the sky. It was a brilliant blue, with billowy clouds, the likes of which she had never seen before. She remained in awe at the beautiful display of nature before her.

The sailing was mostly smooth. There were only two days of storms, when the ship's rocky movements caused Fanny to feel a little seasick. She stayed in bed those days and quickly recovered afterwards.

After two weeks, the S.S. Nordan arrived in New York. Everyone lined up at the ship's rail to see the Statue of Liberty come into view. Shouts of joy rang out from everyone. Hopes were high. The ship docked, and the passengers waited for further instructions.

The steerage passengers had to line up in groups to pass through the Ellis Island Customs and Immigration port. But first and second class passengers were interviewed on the ship by Immigration officials, and the medical exams were conducted on the ship as well.

Fanny passed her inspection and medical exam, and in a few hours her passport was stamped for entry into America. She was then allowed to leave the ship. Malci had offered a place for Fanny to stay that night with her family, since she couldn't get a train ticket to Cleveland until the next day. Fanny was grateful. By now she had become part of the family, and Rachel and Herman adored her.

Fanny waited on the dock for her steamer trunk, which the porter brought down. She stayed there until Malci and the children appeared. "Come," said Malci. "Sol is waiting for us at the pier."

When Malci saw Sol, she ran up to him, and they embraced as though they hadn't seen each other for a very long time. Herman ran up to his papa and hugged him too, but Rachel was a little shy. She had never met her papa before, although with a little coaxing she quickly warmed up to him.

"This is Fanny." Malci told Sol. "She was our cabin mate, and we've become best friends. The children adore her. I told her she could stay the night with us. She is traveling to Cleveland as soon as she can get a train ticket."

"You're so welcome, Fanny. I see you kept my family company on their journey. Come, let's go."

Sol helped carry the luggage. He hired a carriage, and accompanied Fanny and his family to the small apartment in Brooklyn that would be Malci's new home.

The next day, Sol took Fanny to the train station to help her purchase a ticket. There was a train leaving that evening, which would arrive in Cleveland the next afternoon. Fanny was excited to be so close to her final destination. She wired Arthur her arrival time. He had promised to meet her at the station.

The next day, after bathing, Fanny prepared herself for the last leg of her journey. She put on a white blouse that buttoned up to her neck, along with the striped skirt and jacket Mama had sewn for her. Then she laced up the shoes her brother Samuel had made for her. Looking in the mirror one more time, she smoothed her skirt with her hands. Now she was ready for the final part of her journey. Sol, Malci, and the children accompanied her to the train station early that evening. Sol carried Fanny's steamer trunk. The children hugged her good-bye.

"Thank you. *A dank, a dank.* You have made my journey to America so joyful," Fanny told Malci.

"Good-bye, Fanny. We will miss you. Please write to us when you get settled."

Fanny had stepped onto the train in Odessa a nervous and excited young girl. She stepped off the train in Cleveland a confident young woman with many worldly experiences. It was September of 1901. Fanny was seventeen, almost eighteen, and about to embark on her new life in America.

Fanny and Mabel, circa 1906

Fanny in Cleveland, circa 1919

The Girls: Sylvia, Henrietta, Loretta, Mabel and
May, circa 1916   (from left to right)

Bernard in a WWI soldier
uniform, circa 1919

Bernard and his kittens

Bernard happy on his tricycle after getting his nose smashed

Bernard and his sisters: Bernard, Sylvia, Henrietta,
Loretta, May, Mable, circa 1920 (from left to right)

Fanny and Bernard 1925   Fanny and Henrietta, circa 1922

Fanny sitting, Loretta, May, Mabel, circa 1922 (from left to right)

Hyman and Bernard, circa 1924

Hyman with Bernard, circa 1925

Hyman and Bernard, circa 1928

The Twins: May and
Mable (left to right)

Loretta and Bernard, circa 1924

Loretta and one of her many dogs in front
of her store on Central Ave.

Bernard in front of Fanny's General Store, circa 1928

Henrietta in front of Fanny's store, circa 1927

Henrietta with one of
her many boyfriends

Loretta and Henrietta, circa 1925

Henrietta, Sylvia, Loretta and their dogs (from left to right)

Fanny and Bernard, with Fanny's first
Grandson, Matthew, circa 1931

Chief and Joe Stowers at Loretta's café
on Central Avenue (from left to right)

Sylvia, May, Belle Whitman, Henrietta, 1929   (from left to right)

PART II

America

Who will say the Kaddish?

CHAPTER 1

Settling In

"FANNY, FANNY, OVER HERE!" FANNY heard a familiar voice and looked around. Arthur was coming toward her with open arms.

"Arthur!" she shouted. They embraced heartily.

"I'm so glad to see you. Let me get a good look at you. You look so grown up!"

"Yes," she replied, "and you do too."

"Come, we'll take the trolley home." Arthur picked up Fanny's steamer trunk and led the way.

Fanny followed him outside the train station, where horse-drawn trolleys were waiting to pick up passengers. On the ride home, Arthur had a million questions for Fanny. He wanted to know how her journey went, how Mama and Papa were doing, how the kids were, how Anna and her family were getting along—so many questions!

"The Russian soldiers came back looking for you, Arthur, but Papa told them you had gone to America. They came back twice."

"Thank God I am here," Arthur sighed. "How are Parush and Maya doing? And Durga and Roman? I owe my life to them."

"Durga never came back to Gav Gubernia after that summer. I missed her terribly."

The trolley paused at a busy street corner. Arthur told Fanny this was their stop. He helped Fanny down, and then carried her steamer trunk.

"Our home is just down the street. Follow me. I can't wait to show you."

Arthur led the way to a four-storey apartment building on a small, tree-lined street. "There are mostly Jewish immigrants in the apartment building. I am sure you will make many acquaintances. We are on the second floor. The Synagogue is on the next street over."

Fanny followed Arthur up the dimly lit stairs.

"Here we are." Arthur opened up the door with his key. "I was able to rent a one bedroom apartment. You can sleep in the bedroom, Fanny, and I will sleep on the bed in the living room."

Fanny stepped into the apartment. It smelled musty. There was a single large room with a coal stove on one side. Next to it was an ice box, and next to that was a sink with a pump for running water. A small wooden table and chairs were in the middle of the room. On the other side of the room was a bed where Arthur would be sleeping from now on. There was a small side-table where he had placed the two Sabbath candlesticks Mama had given him. The apartment had a small water closet with a toilet, a water pitcher and basin, as well as a tub for bathing. Fanny walked into the bedroom. It was small, but it was all hers. There was a single bed with a little table next to it and an armoire for her clothes. Arthur put the steamer trunk down at the foot of the bed.

"Here you are Fanny. Home at last!" He hugged her affectionately. "I'm so glad you came. I know you'll grow to like it here. I have to go to work early in the morning. I leave at six o'clock and return at four. You might want to take a walk around the neighborhood tomorrow. I'll leave money on the table for you to buy some food. There is some coal in the bin, so you can start a fire in the stove." Arthur demonstrated how the coal stove turned on.

"I spend the Sabbath with the Shaw family. They are my great friends. I met their son, Hyman, on the ship coming over. He has two sisters, Susan and Ada. You'll love them, I know it. Now let's eat something and take rest. You must be tired."

After dinner, Fanny and Arthur spoke of many things. Arthur wanted to hear about home, but he also wanted to orient Fanny to life in America. Fanny wanted to know what happened to Arthur's *payot*. He told her he cut it off during the ship's voyage, in the middle of the ocean. It felt right, and he hadn't regretted it since. After a while Fanny excused herself and retired to her room. She had never had her own bedroom before, and wasn't sure if she would get used to it. But tiredness overcame her. She unpacked her nightgown from her steamer trunk and put it on. After folding her clothes, she lay down on the bed. And before she knew it, she fell fast asleep.

The next morning, Fanny took a bath and then got dressed to go out. She wore a long, dark blue skirt and a white blouse that buttoned up to her neck, and wound her brown shoulder-length hair in a bun at the top of her head. After eating the breakfast Arthur had left for her, she decided to put away her clothes in the large oak armoire that took up a whole corner of her new bedroom. She opened up her steamer trunk and brought out the tea cup and saucer Mrs. Rosenthal had given her for reading tea leaves. Admiring the set one more time, with its attractive gold rim and three pretty pink roses on each side, she carefully wrapped the cup and saucer in two separate cloths. Then she placed them back in the trunk along with the deck of hand-painted playing cards Kalisara had given her. Then, after sweeping her room and tidying it up a bit, she decided to step out to get acquainted with her new neighborhood. The fall air was a bit nippy, so she wrapped a knitted shawl around her shoulders.

Fanny was immediately surprised to see so many shops. First, she went into the bakery shop. She smiled as she smelled the fresh aroma of baked challah, rye bread, and onion bagels. There were cookies and decorated cakes, the likes of which she hadn't seen before, and a sweet snack made of sesame seeds, called *halvah*.

Next to the bakery shop was the kosher butcher shop, where you could order any cut of meat. You could also buy eggs there. She noticed a man behind the counter in a slightly blood-stained white apron. He smiled at her. Fanny was shy to speak, because her English was not yet very good.

The fruit and vegetable market was next to the butcher shop. Arthur had told her that milk, cheese, and other dairy products were delivered to their door. You would just leave your empty milk bottles at your door with a note, and the milkman then replaced them with fresh bottles. This was a novel idea for her. She marveled at how all the necessities of life were so close to the apartment.

Across the street was Levin's General Store. Fanny was curious about it, and so she went in. The general store had lots of different kinds of items for sale. There were hats and gloves for workmen, cigars and cigarettes, tools, coveralls, bolts of cloth to purchase for sewing clothes, ribbons and bows, needles and thread, tools, nails and screws, glass jars, cast-iron teapots, cooking pans—and candy! There was also a new kind of candy Fanny had never seen before. It was a package of caramel-coated popcorn with a sailor on the front, called "Cracker Jack." There were sacks of flour, saltine crackers in a tin box, baking powder, a hand-grinder to grind coffee and another one to grind peanuts. Fanny wasn't sure what coffee was, but the store also had tea for sale. She was glad for that. She was going to need tea leaves. She spent a long time looking around at all the items in the general store.

"*Shalom,*" she said to the store clerk.

"*Shalom,*" he replied in Yiddish. "I haven't seen you before. Are you new here?"

"Yes, I just arrived from Russia. My name is Fanny Lusher. I am Arthur's sister. Do you know him?"

"Yes, he is a customer here. Are you looking for work?"

"I can work."

"Good. I need someone to open the store for me at six in the morning, Monday to Friday, to stock inventory and sell goods until I arrive at eight. Would you be able to do this? I pay 30 cents an hour. You can stay until noon to help. You'll get $1.50 a day. That's $7.50 per week."

"Yes, I'd be pleased to help out. That would be fine, thank you," Fanny replied courteously, careful to show proper outward reserve.

But inwardly, Fanny was quite excited. She had gotten a job the first day she arrived! She couldn't wait to tell Arthur.

The store clerk was a man in his forties. He wore a long-sleeved shirt, which was pin-striped and had black elastic bands just above the elbows. Red-and-black leather suspenders held up his trousers. He had rosy cheeks, brown curly hair, and he wore a dark brown yarmulke.

"I am Yacob Levin. Pleased to meet you. I took over the store from my father when he died. Come back tomorrow at nine in the morning, and we'll go over what you need to know."

"Thank you. Thank you. *A dank. A dank.* Until tomorrow," Fanny replied, and she left the store.

Fanny was even more excited now, as she continued exploring her new neighborhood. She was happy her work would finish at noon. That way, she would have time to keep the apartment clean and have dinner ready for Arthur when he came home. She realized she would need to take English lessons to improve her ability to speak with customers, and her new schedule would also give her time to study.

As she walked along the street, she noticed some dogs sleeping on the side of the road. There were a few horse-drawn carriages that passed by, and some peddlers with their carts. There were also several neatly dressed women on the street who were going in and out of the shops with their baskets.

Then she remembered that Arthur had told her the Synagogue was on Euclid Avenue. She walked over to the next street, where she found a simple brick building with a Star of David above the door. She noticed a smaller building next to the Temple, which had a sign in front that read: "B'nai B'rith of East Cleveland." The B'nai B'rith was a Jewish service organization that specialized in helping newly arrived Jewish immigrants to settle. Fanny approached the office. There she found two women behind two rolltop wooden desks.

"*Shalom,* may we help you?"

"*Shalom.* My name is Fanny Lusher. I'm new to America, having just arrived a few days ago from Russia. I'm exploring my new neighborhood. My brother is Arthur Lusher. He told me you may offer English classes here."

"Welcome. Welcome, Fanny. Yes, I believe we can set you up with one of our volunteers to help you learn English. You may be surprised to learn that there are a lot of words in Yiddish that are similar to English words. Do you live nearby?"

"Yes, just one block over."

"Good. We have an English class for newly arrived immigrants. It meets at six o'clock on Monday and Wednesday evenings. Will you be able to attend?"

"Yes, I would like to. I work in the mornings, and my evenings will be free." Fanny was enthusiastic at the prospect of learning English. She was determined to study hard and learn quickly, and couldn't believe how well everything was going for her.

She thanked the women and went home. Realizing it was time to start dinner for Arthur, she stopped at the butcher shop and bought some chicken to cook. This turned out to be a lot easier than catching, killing, and plucking the chicken! Then she went to the vegetable market and bought some cabbage, carrots, and beets.

It was Tuesday. She would start her new job the next day, working in Levin's General Store, and would also begin her English lessons. Shortly after she got home, the ice man knocked on the door to deliver a fresh block of ice for the ice box. She had never had an ice box before, but she quickly got used to the idea of keeping food fresh for a couple of days. At home there was a metal box outside, where they kept their meat. The Russian winter near Odessa was mild, but cold enough to keep the meat frozen for a few days.

When Arthur came home, dinner was ready and the house was clean. Relieved that he didn't have to prepare anything for himself, he was beginning to see the wisdom of having Fanny there to help him.

"Arthur, I got a job today with Mr. Levin at his general store! And I stopped at the B'nai B'rith to inquire about English lessons. They start tomorrow night!"

"That's wonderful, Fanny. It will be good for you to make a little money of your own."

"Yes, I can help you with the rent now. It will take a burden off your shoulders."

"I knew you would like America, Fanny. If you work hard, you can accomplish many things. There's a lot of opportunity here. And as more immigrants come, there will be more jobs. Everything is changing so fast. They say horseless carriages will be commonplace before too long, and the Wright brothers are building and testing machines that can fly!"

"Arthur, let's write to Mama and Papa and let them know how well everything is going for us here. They will be so relieved to know."

Fanny hadn't gone to school, so she didn't write Yiddish or Russian well. Shortly after Arthur started going to the yeshiva, he began to teach her how to read and write, as well as how to count and write numbers. Now that she was living in America, she couldn't wait to learn English, the language of her newly adopted country. Arthur got out a pen and paper, and the two of them composed a letter to their parents. They wrote that Fanny had arrived safely—and that she already had a job!

When they finished, Fanny remembered that she had promised to write to Moshe and Lillian in Hamburg, as well as to Malci and Sol in Brooklyn.

"Can we write two more letters, to let them know I arrived safely? Moshe and Lillian were so kind to both of us."

"Of course, Fanny. Let's do it."

And so, Arthur and Fanny composed two more letters to their dear friends.

"Fanny, there is a post office three blocks away. You can post the letters tomorrow, before your work."

Fanny felt proud of herself. She had accomplished much in one day. Retiring to her room, she soon fell asleep.

After getting up the next morning, Fanny bathed and got dressed. She combed her hair and pinned it up, then ate a breakfast of lox and bagels. She grabbed her shawl and went off to the post office, where she mailed the letters they had written to Mama and Papa and to their friends.

Then she walked over to her new job at Levin's General Store.

"Good morning, Mr. Levin," Fanny smiled as she greeted him.

"Good morning, Fanny. It's good you've come. We have much to do."

Fanny listened attentively.

"The first thing I want you to do when you come to work in the morning is to sweep the floors, dust, and tidy up the shelves. Next, look around and make sure the shelves are neat and well stocked. If we are low on any items, resupply the shelves from the extra stock." Mr. Levin showed Fanny where various items were kept in cabinets underneath the shelves and in the back room.

"If we are low on any items," he continued, "write them down so I can place an order. Some of the items come from far away, and the sooner we can order them the better off we are. Take note of how the shop is set up. Hardware and tools are on the right side; millinery, thread, needles, and cloth are in the middle. Groceries are on the shelves and candy is at the checkout counter. Customers get attracted to the candy and buy some as they pay for their items. I will come to work by eight o'clock, and the doors will open for business. I will leave you to open up on your own when you learn how to make and record the sales, and also learn how to use the cash register."

Excited about her new job, Fanny pledged to herself to be a good student and learn quickly. That day, she stayed at the store until noon, after which time she went home and ate lunch. Then she cleaned up the apartment and planned for the evening meal.

CHAPTER 2

A New Language

ON WEDNESDAY NIGHT, FANNY WENT to her first English class at the B'nai B'rith. After entering the room, she sat down at an empty desk and waited with six other students for class to begin. Molly Isaacson, the instructor, warmly greeted each of the students as they entered the classroom. An attractive twenty-three-year-old woman, Molly had been born in Cleveland and spoke perfect American English, which she had learned in school—for she was a public high school graduate! In addition, she spoke Yiddish, as that was the language her parents spoke at home. Her parents had immigrated to America in 1877 from Lithuania, which was under Russian rule at the time. They had faced the same pogroms against the Jews that threatened Fanny and Arthur as they were growing up. Molly had light brown hair and a trim figure. She wore a light-blue long skirt with three rows of darker blue ribbons sewn at the bottom. Underneath the matching jacket was a long-sleeved cream-colored blouse that had two rows of ruffles running down the front, along the buttons. When she first came into the room, she had taken her hat off and set it on one of the clothing hooks. Fanny liked Molly right away, and they soon became good friends.

"Good evening," Molly started in English. "We are going to learn to read, write, and speak American English. We will not be speaking

Yiddish in class, only English. First, I will ask each of you to stand up and tell us your name and where you've come from."

After these introductions, Molly went on, "Very good. I see that most of you are from Russia. Now we will start with the First Reader in the Horace Mann series. Horace Mann was an American educator from Massachusetts who believed in equality of education—that is, for boys *and* girls, as well as for all strata of society."

Molly gave each student a beginner's reading book. Beige-colored, its hard cover had a picture of an elephant walking in front of a red semi-circle. The title of the book was "First Reader."

Fanny felt goose bumps as she opened up the first pages of the book. Now she knew she would soon be able to read English. Molly went over the English alphabet and how to pronounce each letter. As a homework assignment, she asked her students to write and practice pronouncing the letters. Class was then dismissed.

Fanny soon developed a routine of going to work in the morning and attending English classes on Monday and Wednesday evenings. She would study in the afternoon and then cook and clean while reviewing what she had learned. On Friday nights, while saying the prayers, Fanny and Arthur would light the Sabbath candles in the brass candlesticks Mama had given to Arthur. On Saturday they would go to Synagogue, where Arthur had introduced Fanny to the Shaws. Mrs. Shaw liked Fanny very much, and Hyman's sisters liked her too.

Fanny was a quick learner, and her English improved significantly. After a few months she could read simple stories and write well. Mr. Levin was now letting her open up the store on her own. Her natural business and sales skills were developing as she engaged customers courteously and learned how to help them. While learning how to sell products, she also learned how to use the cash register and how to keep track of and record sales. As she became familiar with the different suppliers of the stock, she began to place the orders. Mr. Levin was quite pleased with her progress.

One day, Molly invited Fanny over for tea. It was the day before Fanny's eighteenth birthday.

"Tell me about your hometown and your family," Molly started.

"I come from Gav Gubernia, near Odessa. My father is a shoemaker, and my mother makes cloth. We lived near a Gypsy camp, where I learned to read playing cards from Kalisara, a Gypsy woman. My friend Durga and I studied for a long time, until the Gypsy camp broke up two winters ago."

"That's fascinating, Fanny. I've heard about that. It seems card readings are popular in the old country, as is telling fortunes with tea leaves. Do you read tea leaves too?"

"Yes, I learned that from Mrs. Rosenthal, one of our neighbors."

Fanny learned that Molly had been engaged, but her fiancé had been a soldier in the Spanish-American war. He contracted yellow fever in Cuba and was sent home, where he died from complications of the disease shortly thereafter. Molly was a very young girl at the time, and had not yet recovered from the shock.

One day, Molly asked Fanny if she could help her neighbor, Mrs. Goldman, who was distressed over her young son, Herman. She had suffered the loss of her older son due to tuberculosis, and now her younger son wanted to join the army. Molly was wondering if Fanny could do a card reading for Mrs. Goldman, to allay her fears. Fanny agreed. She was eager to get out the playing cards and reconnect to their energy.

"Mrs. Goldman can pay you. Will you accept 25 cents for your reading?"

"That's generous," agreed Fanny. "Ask her to come over on Thursday afternoon at two o'clock."

Thursday afternoon arrived. Fanny had prepared for the reading. She went to her steamer trunk to get out the hand-painted playing cards Kalisara had given her. As she took them out of the special cloth she had wrapped them in, she thought of Kalisara. Then she put a fresh decorative cloth on the kitchen table. She lit a candle and placed some apples in a bowl. Soon she heard a knock at her door.

"Good afternoon, Mrs. Goldman, do come in. You are most welcome."

Mrs. Goldman was an attractive woman in her late thirties. She came in and removed her bonnet. She seemed a little nervous.

"Please sit down," Fanny offered her a chair at the kitchen table. "Would you like some tea?"

"Yes, thank you."

Fanny chatted with her as she prepared and boiled the tea. She asked about her husband and family. She had a natural way of putting people at ease, and by the time the tea was served, Mrs. Goldman was more relaxed.

Fanny began, "Now, I understand you have a question deep in your heart. You do not have to tell me your concern—the cards will. First take three deep breaths. Pay attention to each breath, coming in and going out." As the two women sat quietly, listening to their breath, Fanny thought first of her friend Durga. She then entered into that space of silence Kalisara had spoken of.

When the two women opened their eyes, Fanny asked Mrs. Goldman to shuffle the cards and place the deck on the table and cut the deck in two. After this, Fanny took the top card and placed it in the center of the table. It was the Queen of Spades. *This represents a woman in distress,* Fanny realized. *Let's see what comes next,* she thought to herself.

Fanny placed the next card down, and the next, and the next, until she completed the Wagon Wheel spread. She closed her eyes, touching that place within her own being from which all possibility springs forth: the seed of consciousness. Then the elements of Mrs. Goldman's life, as represented by the cards that appeared in the reading, began to unfold before her. It was as if she was looking at a snowflake under a microscope.

"I see that you are someone who is living with a lot of grief over the past, and that you are concerned about the future of a loved one, a young man. Know that what happened in the past was not a mistake, but what was ordained to be. The soul of the young man in question cries to serve the greater good. He will enter the armed services, but due to some unforeseen circumstance, either an illness or a wound, he will be honorably discharged. After some time he will enlist in civil service, perhaps something like the police department. In this way he will be fulfilled in serving the greater good of the community in which he lives. You will be blessed with grandchildren."

Mrs. Goldman was taken aback. She blinked a few times, as if to take in what was said. She was equally relieved and confused, but slowly she noticed that an underlying feeling of doom was lifted. She could breathe again!

When she was finally able to speak, she said, "Thank you, Fanny. This was very special. I can now go forward, feeling certain that whatever happens will end well. This is a relief. Thank you, thank you again and again."

Mrs. Goldman left a quarter in the porcelain bowl Fanny had put out by the door. Fanny thanked her for coming. After Mrs. Goldman left, Fanny sat down and closed her eyes for a few moments, envisioning the wooden table Kalisara had placed under the trees in the forest of Gav Gubernia.

Word got out that Fanny was good at fortune card and tea leaf reading, and in a short time many different kinds of people were coming to her for a myriad of problems. She became well known as someone you could go to for a consultation, and soon became the community seer. Fanny was so thankful to her teachers, Kalisara and Mrs. Rosenthal, for imparting these gifts. She knew it wasn't her own doing, but it seemed to her as though the answers were coming from her teachers and passing through her. It was more a feeling of gratitude than accomplishment. The practical result, however, was that Fanny now had a sizeable supplemental income. She also met a lot of different people and made many friends. There was a tide of Jewish immigrants coming to Cleveland at that time, and many of them had left family members back home. They all had secret longings and a wish to know how things would turn out for them.

Arthur was happy that Fanny was able to earn her keep, because he wanted to save money to send for their younger brother Samuel, who would soon be facing the harsh reality of conscription into the Tzar's army. Fanny felt the same way, and she helped with expenses as much as she could while also contributing to the fund to bring Samuel to America.

As time went on, Fanny's English became very good, although she still had a strong Russian-Yiddish accent. And from Mr. Levin she came to learn all the aspects of managing a general store. She had a natural ability for business, and a keen sense of the human spirit.

CHAPTER 3

Fanny and Hyman

A FEW MONTHS AFTER FANNY's arrival in America, Mrs. Shaw invited Fanny and Arthur for Sabbath dinner. It was winter. Fanny put on her red wool coat and the matching knitted hat, scarf, and gloves that Anna had given her for keeping warm. There was a light snow coming down. While they were walking to the Shaw home, Fanny marveled at the beauty of the snowflakes as they fell into the beam of the street lamps. Each flake seemed illumined in the glow of the light, reminding her of the snow globes at Mr. Levin's store. When she would turn the globe upside down and back up again, she could watch the flakes scatter and then slowly settle to the bottom of the globe. Fanny was now aware of each step she took. She noticed the snowbanks piled on the sides of the walkway. The moonlight was shining on them, reflecting rainbow-colored ice. She heard the "click clack" sound of hooves as horse-drawn carriages passed by. And as the light snow settled on the city in the dusk of the early evening, the world seemed especially quiet.

"Welcome, welcome," Mrs. Shaw smiled as she opened the front door to greet her guests. "We are so glad to have you."

"Thank you for inviting us, Mrs. Shaw," Arthur and Fanny replied in unison.

Mrs. Shaw took their coats and hats and placed them on the clothing rack. "Come in. Come in. You know Mr. Shaw, Susan, Ada, and, of course, Hyman." Fanny shook hands with the family members, one by one. When it was Fanny's turn to greet Hyman, their eyes met and locked in place for a few moments. Then, in embarrassment, Fanny quickly looked down and Hyman looked away.

"Oh," Mrs. Shaw interjected, noticing their awkwardness, "Let's light the Sabbath candles and sit down to eat. I've cooked a marvelous dinner and bought challah and coconut bars from the Jewish bakery in town."

As the family gathered around, Mrs. Shaw covered her head with lace. She lit the Sabbath candles and prayed:

בָּרוּךְ אַתָּה יְיָ אֱלֹהֵינוּ מֶלֶךְ הָעוֹלָם

Barukh atah Adonai, Eloheinu, melekh ha'olam
Blessed are Thou, O Lord, our God, King of the universe

אֲשֶׁר קִדְּשָׁנוּ בְּמִצְוֹתָיו וְצִוָּנוּ

asher kidishanu b'mitz'votav v'tzivanu
Who has sanctified us with His commandments and commanded us

לְהַדְלִיק נֵר שֶׁל שַׁבָּת: (אָמֵן)

l'had'lik neir shel Shabbat. (Amein)
to light the lights of Shabbat. (Amen)

Fanny closed her eyes and listened intently to Mrs. Shaw reciting the Sabbath prayer. In her heart she felt the full impact of the prayer saying to her: *I remember with all my heart the Lord, Our God, the God of this world who has given us life, who has protected us, who has brought us here to this moment, and who has given us this day of rest, so that we can gratefully Remember and Observe.*

The Sabbath meal was delicious. It reminded Fanny of Mama's home cooking. After dinner, Arthur, Hyman, and Mr. Shaw went to the parlor to talk. Fanny and the girls were chatting with Mrs. Shaw in the dining room while helping her to clean up. They talked about their struggles to learn English. The girls were both attending public school. They asked Fanny about her family and how she liked America. Fanny felt comfortable right away with the Shaws, and she sensed a strange feeling of kinship with Hyman.

Perhaps it's because Arthur and Hyman are such good friends, she thought. Now and then, they exchanged glances over the dinner table or across the room.

At the end of the evening, Fanny and Arthur thanked the Shaws and left to go home.

Fanny continued working at Mr. Levin's store and studying English. She had many clients for tea leaf consultations and telling fortunes with playing cards. At Chanukah time, Mrs. Shaw invited Arthur and Fanny back to celebrate with their family.

"Hello, Fanny," Hyman summoned up the courage to break the ice. "I've been thinking about you a lot lately. I enjoy your company. Do you think Arthur would allow me to ask you to go for a walk with me some time?"

"I don't think that is a problem," responded Fanny. "Arthur could accompany us." Hyman was beside himself, as Fanny signaled to him that she would like to spend more time with him too.

And so the weekly walks began. Hyman came courting to Fanny's door, and Arthur would accompany them on their walks.

This was a new feeling for Fanny. She felt her heart skip a beat when she saw Hyman, who was a tall, handsome man with kind eyes and fine features. Fanny was eighteen, and Hyman was two years older. They were comfortable together and could have fun whatever they did, or even if they did nothing at all.

This went on for some time, and one sunny June day, Hyman called at Fanny's home for their weekly outing. He was dressed in his only suit, freshly pressed for the occasion. When Fanny answered the door, he handed her a lovely bouquet of white carnations.

"These are for you," he said with a big smile.

"Thank you, Hyman. They're beautiful." Fanny went to find a glass vase and filled it with water from the kitchen pump. After carefully arranging the flowers, she set them on the table. "Please sit down. Would you like some tea? I just boiled a pot of water."

As they drank their tea, Hyman inquired, "Where is Arthur?"

"He went out to get the paper. He'll be right back."

"Fanny, today I want to take you on a picnic to Euclid Beach Park. We can sit at the lake and enjoy the cool, refreshing air. On the way to the streetcar, we can stop at the bakery to get some bread, and then at the butcher shop next to it we can get some meat and cheese. When Arthur gets back we'll be on our way. Would you like that?"

"Yes, very much! This is a fine day for a picnic. I'll get ready."

Fanny went to find her picnic basket, her plates and utensils, and a table cloth to spread out on the ground. She had been working hard this past week and was glad for the opportunity to get out and have some fun.

Soon after Arthur returned, they all left for a day at the lakeshore. She loved being with Hyman as he made her feel genuinely cared for, and she always looked forward to their weekly outings. She also loved the close relationship he and Arthur shared. It was sweet to watch how they often teased each other in an endearing way.

When they arrived at the park, they set everything up and sat down together. As Fanny looked out across the cool air of Lake Erie to the horizon, she watched a few white clouds form and dissolve. She listened for the gentle lapping of the waves upon the shore. She loved just relaxing by the lakeside—something that was unimaginable to do back home!

After lunch, Hyman asked Fanny if she wanted to go for a stroll along the boardwalk that ran parallel to the shore. Fanny agreed.

Just a few minutes into their leisurely stroll, Hyman boldly began to speak. "Fanny, you know I think the world of you. I admire you in so many ways!"

"And I, you!" she responded.

Hyman's hands began to shake and his voice quivered. "If Arthur agrees to it, and if you, of course, agree, will you marry me? I would be the happiest man if you would say yes."

"Oh," Fanny uttered softly. She looked down in modesty. It didn't take her too long to think about it, as she'd been hoping for a long time that he would ask. "Yes, Hyman, I will gladly marry you!"

Elated at their mutual vow to be together, Hyman tipped his hat to shield their faces from the eyes of others as he leaned into Fanny for a kiss. When their lips pressed together for what seemed like a long time, Fanny felt a tingling sensation from the top of her head down to her toes! After their lips parted, she felt her heart flutter and her cheeks flush. They smiled at one another as they gazed into each other's eyes. Fanny then locked her arm in his, and they went back to tell Arthur of their longing to be married—and to formally ask him for his approval.

They remained engaged until Hyman could earn enough to afford a home for his bride-to-be. Hyman continued his work as a house painter. It was a good job, with steady work in the spring, summer, and fall seasons. In the wet, cold weather of Cleveland, houses had to be repainted every three to five years, and new homes were being built all the time. There was a boom in the population from immigrants moving into the city. They were drawn by the abundance of work offered in the many factories and steel manufacturing plants that were being built on the shores of Lake Erie.

In the early spring of 1903, Hyman and Fanny were married by Rabbi Eliezer in the Euclid Avenue Temple. Mr. and Mrs. Shaw adored Fanny and were delighted by the match. Molly was her maid of honor, and Susan and Ada were the bridesmaids. One of Fanny's clients was a seamstress, and she had sewn Fanny's wedding dress. It was made of beautiful white satin, with long sleeves and a high neckline. The bodice and sleeves were overlaid with lace, and the long skirt had several rows of white satin ribbon sewn along the border. Fanny felt like a queen.

For his part, Hyman looked dapper in his black suit and white shirt. He felt like the luckiest man in the world! He was deeply in love with Fanny, and they made a handsome couple.

While singing the liturgy, the cantor led the procession down the aisle. His voice filled the sanctuary, creating an atmosphere of sanctity and reverence that touched the hearts of all who were present. Hyman waited nervously under the chuppah. When it was Fanny's turn to walk down the aisle, accompanied by her brother, a big smile of happiness broke out on his face. And when Arthur gave Fanny's hand to Hyman, he felt her gentle softness and her eager willingness to embark on this adventure of marriage with him.

The previous year, Fanny and Arthur had sent for their brother Samuel, who arrived during the summer. He was relieved to come to America and was grateful to his brother and sister. He soon found work in Chicago, where he settled after the wedding. Arthur moved to California a year later, where he met his wife and remained for the rest of his life.

Fanny and Hyman bought a small house for their growing family. Fanny continued to work at Mr. Levin's store, and in 1911 she was able to rent and operate her own store on Central Avenue in

East Cleveland. From then on, throughout her life until WWII, she owned and operated a variety of stores. Later on, the family lived in the rooms behind the different stores, and Fanny continued to read tea leaves and playing cards for interested neighbors and friends.

CHAPTER 4
The Children

FANNY EVENTUALLY GAVE BIRTH TO nine children, of which six survived:

Mabel and May, fraternal twin daughters, were born in 1904.

Loretta and Louise, a second set of twin daughters, were born in 1906. Louise died soon after her birth.

Henrietta, a daughter, was born in 1908.

Sylvia, the youngest daughter, was born in 1913.

Fanny gave birth to twin boys in 1915, neither of whom survived.

And finally, a beautiful baby boy named Bernard was born in 1917. He was the pride and joy of Fanny and Hyman, and of all his five older sisters.

Mabel and May

In May of 1904, the year following their marriage, Fanny gave birth to fraternal twin daughters. In remembrance of her own mother, Masha, and in accord with Jewish tradition of taking the first letter of the name of a beloved family member, the twins were named Mabel and May. Fanny had her hands full in taking care of the babies. Hyman's mother helped during the day, when Fanny was working at Mr. Levin's store. Hyman was able to watch the girls in the winter, for during this time he didn't have his own work to do. When the girls were quiet, and Fanny had time to herself, she read playing cards for some of the neighbors. The population of Cleveland was growing by the day, and everyone carried questions of destiny in their hearts.

Mabel, who was born first, was a natural leader; and May, the second born, was content to follow her twin sister around. Mabel grew to be a tall and lanky child. As a young girl and teenager she quickly learned how to cook, sew, and take care of the younger children. She would cut their hair and make sure they were dressed properly and were ready for school. May was shorter and a little stouter than her twin sister. She was a quiet girl. They were the apple of their parents' eye. Fanny was a good, attentive mother. Having taken care of her younger brothers and sisters so lovingly, motherhood came naturally to her.

Loretta

The second-born children were also twin girls, born in 1906. Fanny and Hyman were surprised, but happy. They named the girls Loretta and Louise, after Fanny's own twin sisters back home. Loretta was the stronger of the two babies. Louise was small, only three pounds at birth, and in poor health. She had to remain in the hospital after Loretta went home, and died when she was just two weeks old.

Fanny and Hyman were deeply grieved. Fanny couldn't shake off the quiet sadness that followed her around for many months. As time went on, Loretta proved to be a strong and practical child. She followed her mama closely and was always ready to help. She quickly became Fanny's devoted assistant. At first she learned how to help with the household chores. She was a good student in school, especially in arithmetic. From the time she was ten years old, she helped Fanny in the store, cleaning up and stocking supplies. By the time she was fourteen, she could make orders and ring up sales, and at sixteen she could do the bookkeeping and accounting. She was always ready to protect her mama and sisters against any problem that arose, for she had a tough nature and wouldn't take guff from anyone.

She became a serious, hardworking young woman. After Papa left the house, she took it upon herself to help her mama become successful in her business, so that there would always be enough money to support the family. When she became an adult, she even owned her own café and bar in East Cleveland. And during the Great Depression of the 1930s, she was a "bookie" for the Cleveland racketeers!

CHAPTER 5

Henrietta

HENRIETTA WAS BORN IN 1908. A happy baby, she smiled a lot, had rosy, chubby cheeks, and delighted in her older sisters' antics. As soon as she could walk, she would run around the yard. When she was a young girl, she would play in the street with the neighboring children and jump rope with her friends. She loved candy and all things sweet. In love with life, she found joy in the smallest things, and was always willing to try something new.

In the 1920s she was the first of her sisters to hike up her dress and bob her hair. She loved styling her hair with the curling iron and spending lots of time in front of the mirror. She was a pretty girl with high rosy cheeks, who loved applying makeup and bright red lipstick. Her best friend, Belle Whitman, was a striking young girl with naturally curly red hair. The two of them went to dances together and flirted with the boys. Henrietta always had a lot of boy-friends. Fanny wasn't happy about it, nor about the way in which her daughter met boys. She and Henrietta had many arguments about this, for Fanny had been raised in the old country, where the parents arranged such things, and girls weren't allowed to go around with boys unchaperoned.

"Henrietta, I won't let you go out with those boys! It isn't proper, and you can get into trouble."

"But, Mama," she would argue, "I'm with Belle. All the kids are going to the dances at the Crystal Slipper. They've got live musicians with really good music. *Jazz music!*"

"I don't want you to go, and that's that. *Oy, Gott in himmel!* Oh, God in heaven!"

Fanny was at her wit's end with Henrietta. Never before had she met a child who so disobeyed her parents. She didn't understand this new era of the independent woman of the 1920s. But Henrietta was coming of age in this new time of freedom, in which women had the right to vote and felt like they had shed the shackles of convention.

So, Henrietta had to be clever in devising ways to get out of the house to meet her boyfriends.

To the Movies

One fine Saturday, Henrietta asked her mama if she could take her brother Bernard to the movies. "We'll go see Charlie Chaplin. He'll really like it. That way he won't be in your way while you tend to the store."

"That's a good idea. Here's 40 cents for the tickets and popcorn. Be back by supper time." Fanny was happy when Henrietta took care of her little brother, and she was especially pleased that Henrietta was showing such responsibility.

"Bernard," Henrietta said, trying to hide her excitement, "Get ready. We're going to the movies."

"Yay!" shouted little Bernard. "I love the movies. Will we see cartoons?"

"I'm sure they will have cartoons. They always show Felix the Cat!"

Henrietta went to her room and combed her hair in the mirror, patting down the curls with her hands. Then she put on ruby red lipstick to accentuate the curves in her lips. After putting on a nice dress, she checked the mirror once more and smoothed her skirt with her right hand.

"Come on, Bernard. Let's go. Put your shoes on and grab your jacket." Henrietta helped Bernard tie his shoes, and then helped him put on his jacket.

"Bye, Mama," they shouted as they left the house. The screen door slammed behind them.

Henrietta took Bernard by the hand as they walked down the street. Bernard started skipping, as he was so happy to go out with his big sister Henrietta.

"We'll be meeting a friend of mine who is going with us to the movies," Henrietta slipped into the conversation.

"Who is she?"

"*He* is Jack. We're going to meet Jack at the next corner. Now remember, don't tell Mama. This is just between you and me. If you tell Mama, I won't take you to the movies anymore."

"Okay. Will he play with me?" Bernard inquired, hoping the answer would be yes.

"I'm sure he will."

That satisfied Bernard. As long as he had a playmate, he was happy. Jack was waiting for them at the next corner. Henrietta flashed a big smile at him, and Jack smiled back.

"You look stunning, Henrietta," Jack swooned.

"Thank you, Jack." Henrietta looked down coyly. "This is Bernard, my little brother I was telling you about."

"Oh yes, how are you doing, little fella? My name is Jack."

"Hello. Will you play with me?" Bernard asked.

"Sure. But first we are going to the movies to see Charlie Chaplin."

"And Felix the Cat!" Bernard chimed in.

Henrietta took hold of Bernard's hand with her right hand and held Jack's hand with her left, and the three of them continued to walk down the street to the movie house. Bernard skipped all the way there. They bought the tickets and found three seats. First, Bernard went into the row and took his seat, then Henrietta, and then Jack. Bernard was so thrilled to be at the movies, he never noticed his sister and Jack were holding hands and cuddling throughout the show.

Double Date

The next Saturday afternoon, Fanny, Loretta, and May were at the store. Mabel was upstairs sewing, and Henrietta and Bernard were talking in the living room.

"Will you play with me?" Bernard kept repeating.

"I'd love to sweet pea, but I am going to go out and meet my friend Sol. We planned it for a long time."

Just then, Henrietta looked out the living room picture window and saw Jack coming up the street! Henrietta forgot that she had made a date with Jack for the same time she had made a date with Sol. She thought quickly.

"Do me a favor, Bernard. I see Jack coming, and I have a date to meet my friend Sol. Can you answer the door when he comes and tell him I'm not home?"

"Sure, maybe Jack will play with me."

Bernard watched with glee as Henrietta grabbed her sweater and ran out the back door. She climbed over the backyard fence just as Jack was coming up the front steps.

Ring, ring, chimed the doorbell.

"I've got it," Bernard shouted upstairs to Mabel. Then he opened the door.

"Hi Jack! Do you want to play with me? I've got some marbles."

"Hello, Bernard. Sure, sure." Jack stepped into the house. Bernard ran off excitedly to get his marbles. He came back, out of breath, and threw them all on the floor. He watched all the pretty colored marbles scatter under the table and under the sofa. Their kittens started to chase after them, trying to grab them with their paws.

"Come on," he entreated.

"Sure, Bernard. But I came to see your sister Henrietta. We had a date. Is she home?"

"Nope, she went out. But will you play with me? Please." he begged again.

"Oh," Jack's heart sunk.

Deeply disappointed, Jack told Bernard he'd love to stay and play but that he had a friend to meet at the soda shop just then. Jack left the house feeling downcast and somewhat dejected. His heart couldn't understand how Henrietta would have forgotten about their date. Had he got the time wrong? What went wrong? He wondered.

The Streetcar Stop

When Bernard went out with Henrietta, they always took the streetcar. It was just 5 cents for a ticket to go anywhere in the city, and there were stops every few blocks. One spring day, Henrietta had taken Bernard out to the park and to lunch, and they were waiting at the streetcar stop to go home. Henrietta was a strikingly beautiful girl. She wore the popular flapper dresses of the day, with colorful baubles hanging down her neck in front of her dress. Her hair was short, and she had put rouge on her cheeks and had also applied eye-liner, and lipstick.

Bernard was busy looking down at the sidewalk, counting the cracks in the pavement while they were waiting. Looking up, he noticed a Ford roadster drive by with its top down. To his surprise, the car came to a screeching halt a few feet ahead of where they were waiting. It then backed up and suddenly stopped right in front of them. There was a dashing young man driving.

"Hello, beautiful! Can I take you to where you're going?" the driver confidently blurted out.

"I'm taking my brother home," Henrietta replied.

"My name is Dave. Hop in. I'll take you home. What's your name?"

"Henrietta. And this is my brother, Bernard.

Taking Bernard by the hand, she said, "Come on, sweet pea. Let's get in. We'll get home quicker this way."

Dave got out of the car and helped Henrietta into the front seat. Bernard sat next to her, by the door. He loved riding in a car!

"Where to?"

"63rd and Central."

"Great! Isn't that where Mrs. Shaw's Confectionary Store is?"

"Yes, that's my mother's store."

As they drove up to the store, Dave asked, "Would you like to go out with me to a dance sometime?"

"I'd love to," she replied. "Pick me up this Saturday night at eight o'clock. See you then."

After they got out of the car, Dave drove off, feeling good about Henrietta and about their upcoming date. Henrietta was feeling pretty good too. She often got dates this way, and that's why her mama was not very happy about it.

When Henrietta got older, she got a job at a five-and-dime store. That way, she knew she wouldn't have to ask her mama for money all the time, and she could be freer to do what she wanted. She and Belle would go to the dance halls together. There was the 'Crystal Slipper' and the 'Trianon,' both located on Euclid Avenue. They loved to listen to the bands and flirt with the boys.

Sylvia

Sylvia was born in 1913. She was a pretty girl and fairly quiet. As a child she was studious and liked to play teacher with her one and only pupil, her younger brother Bernard. She liked frilly dresses, and liked to sashay around in them. She also liked to keep up with the latest fashions. When she was ten, she bobbed her hair. At thirteen, she took up smoking cigarettes, which was all the rage at that time. Cigarettes were readily available at Fanny's store.

Shortly after graduating high school, Sylvia married Sanford Pickle, who was enamored with her. It was a whirlwind romance. They married at the start of the Great Depression. Sanford's family owned a bar, so he was away from home every night and would often come back in the wee hours of the morning—that is, when he *did* come home! He then slept all day long, expecting Sylvia to have a meal ready for him when he woke up. Mostly, he just kept to himself and never showed up at family gatherings. Very few of his nieces and nephews ever saw him. This lack of attention drove Sylvia to smoke more, and she washed her sorrows in tanning herself in the summer sun, shopping for clothes, and spending time with her sisters.

CHAPTER 6

Passing the Flame

IT WAS SIX MONTHS AFTER Sylvia's birth that Mrs. Cohen came into the store, looking for Fanny. Fanny was wearing a simple dress and a white apron over her clothes. She was busy bringing inventory from the back of the store to the front and restocking canned goods on the shelves. There had been a run on canned beans and vegetables, as well as ketchup and tomato soup. She was so focused on her work, she didn't notice the new customer at first. Mrs. Cohen waited patiently, looking around the store.

"Are you Mrs. Fanny Shaw?" she inquired.

"Yes, may I help you?" she replied in her Russian-Yiddish accent as she wiped away the dust from the cans on her apron.

"I am Mrs. Cohen. We just moved into the neighborhood from Chicago. I met your brother Samuel at our Temple there, and he recommended that I speak to you."

"Oh, that's wonderful! How is he doing?" Fanny was delighted to hear news about her brother. They rarely corresponded these days. The last time she had seen him was five years ago when the family went to Chicago to attend his wedding.

"His work is going well, and his daughters are growing beautifully. In our conversations he told me that you read cards, and I was wondering if you could help me with a question."

"Most certainly. Can you come to my home at two o'clock next Sunday? I charge 30 cents."

"That's fine. I will be there. Do you mind if I bring my daughter? She has a keen interest in fortune-telling. She's heard stories about it from her grandmother, who came from Warsaw."

Fanny gave her the address. She was always happy when asked to do readings. Helping others in this way allowed her to reconnect to an inner calm and to the intuitive side of her nature.

When Sunday came, Fanny asked Hyman's parents if they would watch the girls for the afternoon. They were happy to do so, as they enjoyed playing with their granddaughters. After lunch, Hyman bundled them up and took them there on the trolley.

Fanny could now prepare peacefully for Mrs. Cohen's arrival. She swept the floor, tidied the room, and placed a decorative cloth on the table along with a bowl of fruit. From her bedroom cupboard she brought out her hand-painted playing cards and carefully removed them from their cloth case, then put them down on the table in a stack. She sat still for a few moments, preparing herself for the reading by invoking her teacher Kalisara and her dear friend Durga.

At two o'clock sharp Mrs. Cohen knocked on the door. She stood in the doorway with a frail looking young girl by her side.

"Welcome," Fanny said as she opened the door. "Please sit down. Would you like some tea?"

"Yes, thank you."

Mrs. Cohen was sharply dressed in a tailored suit and matching hat. She took off her hat upon entering the home and proceeded to introduce her daughter. Esther, a girl of only sixteen, was modestly dressed in a ruffled blouse and long skirt.

"Pleased to meet you," she said, smiling at Fanny.

After the tea had steeped, the three women sat sipping it as Fanny listened to Mrs. Cohen's story.

"My husband was transferred to Cleveland by his firm. He is an engineer for the American Steel and Wire Company. We have three children. Esther is the eldest."

Esther was a delicate girl, thin, with a pretty face. Her long hair was pulled back and tied in a bow. Fanny detected a seriousness about her that betrayed her years. She gave Fanny an inquisitive, almost hopeful look, as if eager to find something.

Mrs. Cohen continued, "My parents came from Warsaw two years ago. They have relocated with us to Cleveland, and they are settling in very nicely. My sister, however, could not immigrate with my parents, as she is married and has a family back home. Her husband has a high profile job and did not want to leave. His family is also still residing in the Polish Territory. We recently came to find out that she has contracted tuberculosis, and my parents are most concerned for her well-being. Furthermore, there are concerns with her husband and one child. We have come here to learn of their fate.

"Esther has been having vivid dreams lately, in which she sees her aunt, uncle and cousins in peril. She wakes up in the middle of the night, sweating and quite disturbed by these dreams. She sees fire and death in the streets. We have come to dig deeper, in the hope that her fears can be allayed and her nightmares may cease. Ever since Esther was quite young she has been having very clear dreams about our family and the conditions in the world, and some of these dreams have turned out to be true in the end. She is a child who embodies a lot of faith. We are hoping that something will reveal itself in this card reading."

Fanny slowly sipped her tea as she listened to Mrs. Cohen. She thought about the trouble her own family had endured at the hands of the Russian pogroms, and it saddened her.

Fanny was used to hearing all sorts of stories from her clients, and this one did not surprise her. "Very well, would you like to be the querent, Esther?"

"Is it alright, Mother?"

"Yes, if Mrs. Shaw deems it appropriate."

"That would be fine, Esther. I myself began to learn the art of card reading with the Gypsies back home, when I was just about your age. Shall we begin?

"First of all, I would entreat you to sit quietly with your hands folded on your lap. Pay attention to your breathing, and take three full breaths, first in and then out. When you feel ready, shuffle the deck and then cut the stack of cards in two and place the bottom half on top."

The women sat like that for a few moments. Esther closed her eyes and looked as if she were deeply praying. Shuffling the cards as she took in a deep breath, she cut the deck in two and placed the bottom half on top. Fanny turned over the top card to reveal the card that would represent her as the querent. It was the Knight of Spades.

Fanny laid out the next card to the right and then one to the left of the first card, and then others to the top and the bottom of the central card. She continued in this way until she had laid out the full Wagon Wheel spread.

Fanny took a moment to engage the cards within her psyche. First she looked at the gesture of the suits and numbered cards as they were positioned before her. When she closed her eyelids, she could still see them in her mind's eye. They seemed to penetrate deeper and deeper within, until they reached the point where the energy of Kalisara began to speak through her. *The layout of these cards shows the aura of a very intuitive person,* she thought to herself.

Then she began to speak: "I see before me a sensitive person who is very much in touch with her inner voice. These are difficult times for the world and for your loved ones. Europe is currently hanging on tenterhooks, and the outcome of the actions between states of government will affect your dear ones. Your dreams are not just the fanciful notions of a child, but actually bear some truth. If possible it would be good for your family to leave Europe. If this is not possible for them, prayer is the proper tool.

"You will shortly receive a letter from your family, which will explain the current situation. Your aunt will go through a transition in her health, and will be traveling to seek help. In the near future your cousin will be forced to leave home, wearing new clothes. Some, but not all of your family, will be able to travel to America."

Fanny sat back for a moment and closed her eyes to go inside. Before her mind's eye she saw death and destruction in Europe—fighting, suffering, and even all-out war. She knew Jewish people never fared well in such situations. She decided to keep silent so as not to distress her clients. She felt her duty as a counselor was to give hope even in a dire situation, remembering what Kalisara had said: *"Death and destruction are not always bad. There is a time to let go, and sometimes we need to lose something in order to gain another, even better, thing."*

Fanny concluded the session on a lighter note. "Your grandparents will do well here, and will enjoy a long and happy life."

After Fanny stopped reading, Mrs. Cohen sat quiet for a few moments. She didn't quite know what to make of it. She was both relieved and saddened.

Esther instinctively knew all the unspoken parts of the reading. She just nodded her head.

"Mother," she spoke, "I understand what Mrs. Shaw is doing, and I am very attracted to the art of fortune card-reading. If it is alright with you, and if Mrs. Shaw agrees, I would very much like to learn from her how to employ the cards in this way in order to benefit others. I, too, would like to be a fortune teller."

"I don't see any harm in it, and perhaps it will help you in the long run. We will have to ask your father. If he approves," she continued, as she then looked up at Fanny, "and if Mrs. Shaw agrees to it, then you may come for lessons."

Fanny thought about this for a moment. She saw before her a young girl excited to absorb precious inner knowledge. It reminded her of how eagerly she had looked forward to her own sessions with Kalisara, especially with her friend Durga by her side. She felt empathy towards the girl. She also detected within her a sympathetic soul who was naturally attracted to the hidden mysteries.

"Yes, Esther, I will take you on as a student. I see you are ready."

Esther's heart leapt at the thought of studying with Mrs. Shaw.

"Thank you so much for the reading, Mrs. Shaw. We should be going now. We will be in touch," Mrs. Cohen said as she put on her hat and coat. "Come along, Esther."

When the women left, Fanny realized how happy she was to have such a worthy student. She was grateful for the wonderful and inspiring teachers of her own youth. It was only fitting that she would pass on what she had learned. It was true they were no longer in a village in the old country, but now lived in a new world, within a neighborhood of Jewish congregants. A seer's abilities could serve to guide the members of a community, and there were still waves of immigrants who took comfort in this folk wisdom. Curious onlookers were among them, of course, but they too had a sense of the worth of such guidance—or else they would not feel drawn to seek it out.

A few days later, Mrs. Cohen sent word to Fanny that Mr. Cohen had approved of the request for Esther to learn fortune-telling. She also noted that her daughter could be ready for lessons at any time.

Fanny replied to Mrs. Cohen that she was delighted to help and requested that Esther come to the store the following Sunday at two o'clock for her first lesson.

Fanny's store was not open on Sundays, but it offered a quiet place, away from the children. Her own daughters were at home with Hyman. Fanny had prepared the back room of the store for her session with Esther. She covered the table with a lovely cloth Kalisara had given her, put out a bowl of fruit, lit a candle, and brought out her cards.

Esther had walked over to the store from her home. She knocked on the door. Fanny greeted her warmly.

"Come in. Would you like some tea?" she offered.

"Yes, thank you, Mrs. Shaw."

Fanny showed her to the back room and put on the tea kettle.

"You may place your coat on the rack by the door, and then please sit down."

Fanny poured the tea into her special porcelain teacups, which had a ring of gold trim around the rims as well as along the edges of the saucers. A design of three pink roses was painted on the sides of the cups. The bottoms of the cups were white on the inside, as these were the teacups she used for reading tea leaves.

"Tell me about yourself, Esther. What do you wish to know?" Fanny began.

She sighed, and then she began, "When I was nine years old I started having vivid dreams. I didn't know what to make of them and most of them I quickly forgot on waking. But one night I dreamed of an enchanting Light that was brilliant to behold, but it also had a cooling effect. As I stared at this Light it took the shape of a beautiful woman, clothed in shimmering gold. She was radiating love all around her, in all directions, as if she herself were the very rays of the sun. It seemed to me as if she were the Burning Bush of Moses, scintillating with all the glory, all the love, and all the grace of God. When I awoke I lay in bed for a while, immersed in the tremendous feeling of peace and joy.

"Ever since then, many dreams have come. In these I see people, and I come to know of events that eventually take shape. At first I was afraid to tell my mama. I didn't want to speak of such things, for I feared they would disappear.

"But when I came to know of events that affected our family, I began to speak up. Mama didn't know what to make of it and thought it was a child's fantasy that I would outgrow. But the dreams persisted. And when she learned about you from your brother Samuel, she wanted to meet you to see if you could help me shed light on my experiences."

Fanny sat back in her chair as she listened intently. So focused was she on Esther's story, she forgot to drink her tea. While she was listening, she noticed her own thoughts had become silent. She knew that in the old country, in Gav Gubernia, many people had such prophetic dreams. In fact, she had learned about it from her own teacher, Mrs. Rosenthal, who was an expert in dream interpretation.

"Esther," she quietly spoke. "I believe you have been graced with the gift of prophecy. You have a tender, open soul. If you choose, you can now use your gifts to help others through the guidance fortune reading can provide.

"You have one eye in this world and one eye in the next. This is a gift you brought with you from before you were born, and I can help you cultivate it so that you can master the intuitive arts. These arts are used in the old country, among Jewish and Gypsy people alike—card reading, tea leaf reading, dream interpretation, palm reading, reading the stars—there are so many methods that have been devised over the centuries. They arose because people throughout the ages have wanted to know about the worth and meaning of life, about the potential outcome of their endeavors, and about their children and loved ones.

"My own teacher, Baba Kalisara, was a Gypsy woman who simultaneously lived in two realms. She was a free spirit. And just as she was able to light the lamp of knowledge within me, so will I gladly teach you, an eager student, who has asked from the depths of her heart for this wisdom."

And so the lessons began. Fanny taught Esther about the meanings of the cards, their placement in the Wagon Wheel spread, their influence on one another, what the readings can and cannot accomplish, and how to assess each client and their needs. She gave her the basics, the fundamental knowledge upon which card reading is done.

Esther came for her lessons every Sunday at two o'clock. She studied hard, and quickly understood the meanings of the suits and the numbers of the cards. As part of her training, Fanny invited her to observe card readings, and later tea leaf readings, that Fanny did for her clients.

Esther began to spend ever more time with Fanny as her apprentice, and would sometimes help in the store after school. She soon met her children too, and became very fond of them. Occasionally, when needed, she would help Fanny out by watching her daughters. The girls grew to adore her and enjoyed it when she visited. This was a tremendous help to Fanny, who had a store to run and five children to watch. Hyman watched the children when he wasn't working, but he worked long hours when he was painting houses. May and Mabel were ten years old now, and although they could assist a little with their younger sisters, Esther proved to be a big help. Fanny was glad she could count on her.

It was six months before Fanny felt Esther was ready for the next step. Then, one Sunday when she came for her lesson, she noticed that Fanny had lit a candle and set out a bowl of fruit along with a few spring flowers in a glass vase.

"Today we will talk about focus and intention. When you begin a card reading, Esther, you need to create a hallowed space in which to allow the energies of the cards to manifest. After you set up your table and while waiting for your client, sit very quietly and let your mind become still. You can do this by first sitting upright and then focusing on your breathing. Feel your breath as it goes in and out. Pay attention to how it fills and empties your lungs.

"Breath is a mysterious thing. It is the *Ruach Elohim*, the spirit of God, the breath of Life. It is the soul falling again and again into incarnation, into life, into embodiment. As you practice, you will notice the interval between the breaths getting longer—it's almost as if you are unconsciously holding your breath. From that interval, which *is* full potential, all answers spring forth, and the meaning of the configuration of the cards will appear before you."

Fanny encouraged Esther to practice sitting quietly at home every day, which she discovered came very naturally to her. Faithful to Fanny's instructions, Esther endeavored every day to access that quiet place within, that ever abiding eternal presence. She spent many months practicing, until one day she went so deep inside, to that place beyond the mind, where she began to hear Fanny's voice speaking through her explaining the layout of the cards.

After learning how to access the guidance of her teacher from within, she was now eager to begin her own card readings. Fanny encouraged her to practice first on her brothers at home.

As her studies progressed, Esther began to understand the value of her dreams. And as she continued to learn about the gifts of her inner life from Fanny, she was able to integrate her dream visions more easily with day-to-day life. She learned from Fanny how to cultivate her intuition. That year, she blossomed into a sensitive and caring young lady who was empathetic towards others.

At the end of the year, Esther had completed her training with Fanny. Pleased with her student's progress Fanny ordered a special deck of playing cards to present to her for use in her own readings. Esther was quite proud to receive them and knew she would cherish them her whole life. Fanny's work with Esther had come to an end. Esther was now ready to receive clients of her own. She was able to use a combination of knowledge and intuition to unfold the answers to the questions that were put before her through the cards.

By now, the Great War was raging in Europe. Esther's cousin had been drafted into the Russian army. Her aunt sought medical attention for her tuberculosis and for several months was placed in a remote sanitarium outside of Warsaw. She died five weeks after she returned home. Mrs. Cohen and Esther were deeply grieved upon hearing this news.

During this time, Fanny worried about her own family back home. She cherished every letter she received from them.

Then, to her surprise, she discovered she was pregnant again.

CHAPTER 7

The Reason Why Hyman Moved out of the House

FANNY GAVE BIRTH TO TWIN boys in 1915 who did not survive. This was hard for Fanny and Hyman, and they began to argue more about finances and supporting the family. Hyman would not work in the winter, and he did not contribute to the household income during that time. Fanny felt she could not support five daughters on her own *and* a husband who did not work.

Hyman couldn't work in the winter. He just couldn't. His fingers would freeze and the house paint would freeze, and it wouldn't dry properly. No, he couldn't really work in the bitter, cold Cleveland winter. His job was meant to be done in the spring, summer, and fall. In the winter he preferred to sit by the fireplace, read the paper, and smoke his pipe. He helped with getting the girls up and dressed in the morning. He would take them to the park to sled and ice skate on the weekends. He would shovel the sidewalks and the driveway. But no, he couldn't paint houses in the winter—and he didn't feel the need to seek other employment during that time.

Fanny was not happy with this arrangement.

"Hyman," she told him over and over again, "We've got five girls to feed, and coal to buy to heat the house. You've got to work and make some money."

"Fanny," he replied many times, "I am a house painter, and I cannot work in the winter."

They would go back and forth, back and forth, with neither one of them advancing their argument. Finally, exasperated with Hyman, Fanny told him in no uncertain terms to leave the house in the winter.

"I can't afford to feed the children *and* you," she shouted angrily. "You cannot live here when you do not work. You can move back in when you are working. And you can continue to pick the girls up on weekends and take them out during the winter. But you cannot stay here with us."

Fanny was heartbroken. She loved Hyman very much, but she was at the end of her rope. She was working so hard operating her store, earning what she could to feed and raise five children, and she just didn't feel it was right that Hyman would not contribute to the household income in the winter.

And so, two years went by like this. Hyman moved out of the house in the winter and moved back in during the spring time when the new buds started to form on the trees. During the winter he moved in with his parents. His mother was glad to have him because not only did he keep her company, he also kept the stove full of coal, shoveled the walkways, and helped with household chores.

In 1917, the year when little Bernard came along, his parents were no longer living together. They were separated and eventually they divorced. The Great War was still raging, and this was the same year the Bolshevik Revolution took place in Russia under the leadership of Vladimir Lenin. Fanny was worried for her family back home.

Early in 1917 Fanny received the last communication she would ever have with her family in Russia. Eager for news, Fanny quickly tore open the envelope of the letter she had received from home. Papa had written! *"Dear Fanny,"* it began. *"We hope this letter finds you and the girls doing well. We are delighted to hear that you are expecting another child soon. We are praying for a little boy."*

Fanny's heart started to beat a little faster, as she feared the news from home would be grave. She read on.

"The War has caused a lot of problems for us. At first, our Jewish neighbors from the front lines migrated down to Gav Gubernia. We welcomed the newcomers as our own family. But the refugees kept pouring into the village, overwhelming our ability to care for them. The soldiers were not far behind. They forced many of the young men of the village to join the army. Anna's daughter Rachel, who just turned seventeen, was engaged to the schoolmaster's son David. They were to be married this fall, but David was conscripted into the army and taken away by the Russian soldiers. He has not been heard from since. We fear he may not return to us.

"The government is in chaos. There is talk of another revolution led by the Bolsheviks. Many of our people are being forced to move into the interior of the country, away from the front lines, as there is suspicion that the Jews are collaborating with the Germans. There is a lot of animosity towards us, as we are also being blamed for the Marxist uprising. Our villages are ransacked time and again. It is getting harder to get food to eat.

"Lilly and Lana are getting along. Their young children are attending school and growing up quickly. Joseph's family is doing fine. He is still helping me with shoemaking, but is doing the bulk of the work as I am slowing down.

"It's been a while since we heard from Arthur and Samuel. We pray they are prospering. Mama sends her love. She thinks of you every day, and hopes someday the family will be together again.

"May the Almighty God protect us all.

"Your loving Papa"

When Fanny finished reading Papa's letter, she held the pages close to her heart. For a moment's time, in her thoughts, she was back in Gav Gubernia with her family once again, hugging her mama and wiping away her tears.

Soon thereafter, Fanny lost contact with her family back home in the Ukraine. She never heard from them again, although she worried for their safety and constantly prayed for their well-being.

CHAPTER 8

Bernard

BERNARD, BORN IN OCTOBER 1917, was a beautiful baby boy. He was the pride and joy of Fanny and of his sisters. Hyman was proud, too, even though he wasn't living with the family. The girls all took turns holding him, feeding him, and taking care of him. Bernard had a zest for life, and he was a happy, curious, and obedient boy. He, in turn, loved his mother and sisters. He was born towards the end of the Great War, and as a show of patriotism when he was twenty months old, they dressed him in a small soldier's suit, gave him a rifle to hold, and took his picture. Bernard loved being the center of attention, and he wanted to please everyone—so he held still.

All of his sisters adored him, and each played a special role in his life. Mabel sewed clothes for him. She cut his hair and kept him clean and dressed. May followed Mabel around, and would hold Bernard and tell him stories. Loretta protected him by making sure he had enough to eat and was kept safe. Sylvia played school with him. She was the teacher, and he was the reluctant student. He didn't want to sit still. He wanted to run around and play outside. But when Sylvia sat him down to play school, he had to listen! In spite of his resistance, he learned a lot, and was able to skip a grade when he went to public school. But Henrietta—oh Henrietta!—she often took him out to play. Playing was pretty much all little Bernard wanted to do. He liked skipping and running around with the neighbor kids. He was happiest when he was outside, and he loved it when Henrietta took him to the movies or to a dance.

Jumping Rope

One day, Henrietta was playing jump rope with her friends in the driveway. Two girls were on either end of the rope, and one girl jumped in the middle while singing a song. Bernard was then eighteen months old, and just for fun he was running up and down the driveway. He was curious about the game. Henrietta stopped to tease him every now and then. So Bernard thought he'd tease her back by running through the rope just when the girls were jumping.

"Bernard, stop that!" Henrietta appealed.

Bernard thought it was fun, so he kept jumping through the rope. Finally, after being yelled at enough, he sat down on the curb by the side of the house where a cellar window happened to be open. Marcy, one of Henrietta's friends, was so mad at Bernard that she came over to where he was sitting.

"You're such a pest," she cried angrily. And she gave him a shove.

Poor little Bernard fell through the open cellar window and into the basement! He fell on his right side and hit his right shoulder on the two-burner gas boiler that was used to heat and launder the clothes. He bounced off the boiler and landed on the floor.

"Bernard!" Henrietta cried out.

She ran down the cellar steps and picked him up. He was screaming with fear and pain. She asked Marcy to run to the store and tell her mama, and then carried him, crying and yelling, straight away to the hospital. Fortunately, the hospital was on the next street.

Marcy came running into the store, out of breath and looking quite shaken.

"Mrs. Shaw, Mrs. Shaw," she said, "Something terrible has happened to Bernard. He fell through the basement window. Henrietta has taken him to the hospital. Come quick!"

Fanny called out to Mabel, who was at the back of the store, and instructed her to take over while she was gone. With her apron still tied around her neck, Fanny then ran over to the hospital.

"Oh my little baby, oh my little boy," she cried out. Fanny was worried that perhaps he had hit his head and was severely injured. She'd heard about an infant in the old country who died when she was dropped on the floor by a young girl.

"Will he be all right, doctor?" Fanny inquired anxiously.

When Bernard saw his mama he began to cry even more loudly.

It took two people to hold him down while the doctor examined him and determined that his right shoulder bone was broken. While he was screaming, the doctor set his shoulder and then taped his right arm to his body to avoid movement, in order to let it heal. For six weeks Bernard had to endure the uncomfortable bandage. During this time he couldn't move his right arm.

After a few days, Bernard got used to the cast and was soon running around again. Fanny had to watch him more carefully, as his balance was off. When the doctor finally removed the bandage and pulled his little arm away from his body, all the skin was rotted, sweaty, and wet from being tied up for so long. It seemed to him that it took quite a while for the skin to grow back. Fanny put ointment on his arm and kissed him every day until the skin healed up.

Jumping Fences

As Bernard grew a little older, he loved to be outside playing all the time with the neighborhood kids. One day, the boys decided they would go down the block by jumping over the backyard fences, one after another. They were going along, fence-by-fence, when Bernard misjudged a jump and landed on a plate glass window that was leaning against one of the fences. He got a severe cut in his leg. It was bleeding so profusely that he tied a handkerchief around the leg and ran home. He was afraid to tell his mama, and when he reached the house he ran straight to bed.

After a while, Hyman came over to see his son.

"Where's Bernard?" he asked.

"He ran home and went right to bed," Fanny answered. "When I came home from work he was already sleeping."

Hyman went in to see Bernard, to hug and kiss him and cover him up. He found him in bed, whimpering a little. When he removed the cover he saw the gash in his leg, and there was quite a lot of blood.

"What happened, Bernard?" he asked with a worried look.

"I cut myself on a glass window."

"Why didn't you say something?"

"I was scared. I didn't want Mama to know."

Hyman told Fanny, and they called the doctor right away. Dr. Weidenthal came over and examined his leg.

"We'll have to stitch it up. The cut is too deep," he pronounced.

Right there and then he took out a curved needle and thread, and sewed the cut up with seven stitches. Hyman, Loretta, and May had to hold him down, and Fanny held his hand. He was screaming so loud that the cats in the next alley heard him and started to meow, and the dogs started to howl. The doctor didn't use any anesthesia. He just started sewing one stitch after the other.

When the doctor finished his work and left the house, Fanny took Bernard in her arms to calm him down. She began to tell him the story of Goldilocks and the three bears. Bernard was in pain, but he loved it when his mama told him stories. Soon he stopped crying.

When she finished the story, she gave him some chicken soup and sang him to sleep with a Yiddish lullaby.

Fortunately for Bernard, the stitches came out more easily than they went in; and when the time came, he was happy to be rid of them.

Fanny was worried for her little boy. But she was working hard at the store. She depended on Sylvia and Henrietta to look after him during the day.

"Bernard, honey," she would tell him, "please be careful when you are out playing with your friends. And listen to your sisters."

It wasn't that Bernard wasn't listening to his sisters, but he was a little boy, and he liked to run around.

Nosing Around

After a while Bernard was again playing with his friends, Pete and Willie. They had gone to a four-storey apartment building that had long porches in the back, with railings. There were no elevators, and the tenants had to walk up the flights of stairs to get to their apartments. So the boys went over there and decided to play at being construction workers. Pete tied a flat iron, as used in ironing clothes, to a rope. They went to the fourth-floor porch, where they pretended they had to pull the iron up on a pulley. After a while, the boys pretended something was wrong with the load.

"Bernard," Pete said, "something's wrong on the second floor. You go down and check it out."

While he was walking down the stairs to the second floor, Pete let the rope go down to the first floor. And just as Bernard reached the second floor, Pete pulled the iron up to the level of the second floor. He did this just as Bernard was leaning over the railing, pretending to see what the problem was with the load. At that moment, the iron swung out, and then in, and it hit him on the side of his face. It knocked him so hard that he fell down a whole flight of stairs!

He got up and ran home crying, his nose was flattened to the side of his face. Fanny was scared. She rushed him to the hospital on the next street, carrying Bernard who was screaming and wailing all the way.

At the hospital the physician on call took a look at him and realized his nose bone was dislocated. With two nurses holding him down, the doctor grabbed a pair of pliers and inserted it into Bernard's nose. Then he grabbed the nose bone and jiggled it around until it was repositioned. Finally, he took two metal sleeves, one for each nostril, and shoved them up his nose to hold the bone in place. There was no anesthetic. Bernard was kicking and screaming, even louder than before. Fanny felt bad for her son. All she could do was hold him and assure him that things would be alright.

Every two weeks thereafter, they had to go back for checkups. Bernard hated the checkups, because the doctor would remove the metal sleeves to check his nose and then reinsert them. Finally, after eight weeks, the ordeal was over, and his nose bone was healed. Bernard was so happy to be rid of the metal sleeves. He celebrated by riding his tricycle around the block, grinning all the way. Fanny smiled to see her little son happy again.

Luna Park

"Come on, Bernard. Get your jacket. We're going to Luna Park!" Henrietta shouted one day.

"Yay!" Bernard screamed at the top of his lungs. He ran to get his jacket and laced up his shoes. "I'm ready!"

"We're going to meet Belle, Jack, and Buddy, and we'll all have a good time!" she continued.

Luna Park was an amusement park located at East 105th and Woodhill Road. There were all kinds of rides: a Merry-Go-Round with a tiger that you could ride on; a Fun House with a mechanized mannequin of a fat, laughing lady in the front; and a Dance Hall. Bernard especially liked the ride called "Over the Falls." It was a ride with a row boat that went along a track, and at the end of the ride it went down a small hill into a lake, splashing everyone as they went down. Bernard loved the feeling of getting splashed on a hot summer day.

But of all the rides at Luna Park, Henrietta liked best a ride called "The Jack Rabbit," which had a very steep vertical drop. It had the reputation of being the roller coaster with the steepest drop anywhere west of New York and east of Chicago. Henrietta was a daredevil, and she loved it. She loved especially going on the ride with a boy-friend, so she could scream and hold onto him during the drops.

Bernard had so much fun that day! Belle went with him on the Merry-Go-Round, and they all went together on "Over the Falls." They ate a lot of cotton candy and hot dogs, and generally had a good time.

Henrietta was itching to go on "The Jack Rabbit," but couldn't find her friends. They were on the Ferris Wheel, and she just couldn't wait any longer.

"Come on, Bernard. We're going on 'The Jack Rabbit!'"

Little Bernard didn't know any better, so he just followed his big sister, whom he adored, to line up for the ride.

Bernard was only five years old, and wasn't really as brave as Henrietta. "Let's go," she said, as they boarded the car.

Bernard hopped in and held onto Henrietta's hand. He was a little apprehensive about what might happen. The car started to go, at first slowly as it climbed up the hill. Bernard got a little more worried as the car kept going higher and higher. When it got to the top and let rip down the hill, Bernard let out a blood-curdling scream! He felt like his stomach was in his throat, and his heart at the top of his head. He wasn't sure if he was going to be right, ever again.

"Waaaaah!" he screamed. "Henry, Henry, Henry!!!!"

Realizing that maybe she had pushed her little brother too far, she grabbed him to hold onto him—but by then they were at the bottom of "The Jack Rabbit."

As soon as he could, Bernard ran out of the car. He ran as far away as he could go, crying and crying, scared out of his wits. He kept running, until he ran into Belle and Sol. While Bernard was still crying, Belle asked him what happened.

"The Jack Rabbit!" he screamed.

And never again in his entire life did Bernard go on another roller coaster ride.

The Bad Tooth

One day, when Bernard was a little older, his mouth swelled up. It was aching terribly. His mama noticed it and asked Loretta to take him to the dentist. Bernard was afraid to go. He didn't know what would happen.

"I don't want to go," he pleaded.

"But Bernard," Loretta insisted, "the whole side of your face is swollen! You have an infection. Mama asked me to take you to the dentist. So we're going. Put on your jacket."

She helped him with his coat, and then dragged him off by the hand.

"What can we do for you?" the nurse smiled as they walked into the dentist's office. "Oh my, it looks like you have an infection. We'll get you right in to see Dr. Bieber."

Loretta pushed Bernard into the exam room. She sat him down on the chair. Dr. Bieber came in and took one look at him.

"You have a tooth abscess!" he proclaimed. Dr. Bieber got out a pair of steel pliers. Bernard squirmed. There was no Novocain in those days. He just reached into Bernard's mouth and yanked the tooth out.

"Ooowwww!" he let out a big scream. Then, before anyone knew it, he jumped out of the chair, bolted out of the office, and ran as if to save his life the fifteen blocks back home to his mama.

"Mama," he cried, "the dentist pulled my tooth out, the dentist pulled my tooth out!" He was whimpering and crying. Fanny took him into her arms.

"Everything will be all right, Bernard. I will tell you a story." She proceeded. "I will tell you a story about Mary and Morrie, and now my story's begun. I will tell you another about their brother, and now my story is done," she said as she hugged him tight.

Bernard laughed through his tears. "See, you are better already," Mama said. "I'll give you some chicken soup for dinner."

Tom Mix and the Horse Trick

One day, Henrietta took Bernard to the movies to see Tom Mix, the famous cowboy.

"Let's go to the movies, Bernard. We'll see Tom Mix. Do you want to go? Mama said it was okay."

"Yes!" shouted Bernard with glee. "Will we see Felix the Cat, too?"

"Yes," answered Henrietta. "Get your coat on, and let's go."

They put on their coats and left the house.

Henrietta held onto Bernard's hand, and Bernard was joyfully skipping down the street. When they got to the corner, Buddy Berenstein was waiting for Henrietta.

"Hi, Henrietta. Hi, Bernard. Shall we go?"

Bernard liked Henrietta's friend Buddy, and Buddy liked Henrietta—so they all went happily to the movie house. They bought the tickets and candy and took their seats. Henrietta was in the middle, and she took Buddy's hand during the show.

First they showed the cartoons, featuring Felix the Cat. Bernard loved Felix the Cat. He laughed and laughed as he watched the Professor try to take Felix's magic carpet bag. Next came the feature movie with Tom Mix, called "The Last Trail." Bernard sat glued to his seat as he watched cowboy Tom ride his horse across the prairie land and through the Wild West, with American Indians helping him out and the bad guys chasing after him. In one scene Tom was being chased, and his horse was going real fast. He came upon a low-hanging tree branch, and grabbed the branch just as the horse was going under it. He held onto the tree and climbed up into it just as the outlaws were coming up; and they kept going, thinking they were chasing Tom—but in reality it was only a galloping horse.

Bernard loved this scene. He thought about it for a long time after they got home, and for many days after that. He didn't have a horse, but he *did* have a scooter, and so he thought he would try out the stunt on his scooter. He found a tree with a low-hanging branch. He started running on the scooter from the end of the block, and kept on going faster and faster. He could feel the outlaws on his tail until he reached the tree. When he got to the tree branch, he let go of the scooter to grab the branch. He almost had it, but then his hands slipped. He put his hand out to try to stop his fall, but instead landed on his left hand and dislocated his thumb. He ran home crying to his mama.

"Bernard, now what happened?" Fanny asked soothingly.

"I was playing cowboys and I fell off my scooter. My left hand hurts!"

"Let me see it." Bernard held out his hand. Fanny took hold of it very tenderly. She moved the fingers up and down. Then she moved the thumb.

"Ow," cried out Bernard.

"You've sprained your thumb. Let's put a bandage around it to keep it from moving. It'll be alright in a few days."

Fanny carefully wrapped a cloth around the base of his thumb and tied it around his hand. After a few days he was out playing again, but his days as a cowboy had come to an end.

Fanny wasn't prepared for such an accident-prone child. The girls had been easy to bring up. They played quiet games like jump rope, jacks, cards; they played with their dolls. They entertained each other, and they helped in the store. But poor Bernard! He seemed to get into one scrape after another.

Once Bernard healed up, he quickly forgot his trials. He was a good student and made friends easily. He loved staying up late at night, talking with his sisters about all kinds of things. They mostly talked about boyfriends, other girls they knew, dances, and new dresses. Bernard soaked it all in. He loved listening in on "girl-talk." It made him quite sympathetic to women as he grew older.

Learning to Drive

When Bernard was thirteen, he wanted to learn how to drive. No one would teach him. His brother-in-law wouldn't, his mama wouldn't, and there was no one else he could appeal to. About this time, Henrietta, who was now twenty-one, was working as a waitress in a small restaurant. Her boss had a car, and he wanted her to run errands to pick up supplies for the restaurant; and so her boss taught her how to drive. Then he allowed her to take the car home in between the lunch and dinner hours.

Henrietta had an idea to teach Bernard how to drive in her boss's car. In those days there were no driver's licenses.

"Come on, Bernard, I'll teach you how to drive in Mr. Samuelson's car," she told him one day. It was a 1929 Ford.

Bernard got into the driver's seat, and Henrietta sat next to him. She taught him how to start and steer the car. She told him to watch out for other cars on the road, and to always look into the rearview mirror. They proceeded to drive around the streets of Cleveland. Bernard was so happy, for he loved to drive—he loved the feeling of being behind the wheel of a car. He soon became a good driver. And it was because he could drive that he met his future wife.

In 1934, in high school, Bernard had a best friend, Dave Munitz. Dave had a girlfriend, Arlene, but he couldn't take her out because he didn't have a car. Arlene had a girlfriend, Mildred, who didn't have a date. So Dave convinced Bernard to go on a double date. If Bernard would supply the car, Dave would supply the date. Fanny had a car at that time, and allowed Bernard to drive it. So Bernard picked up Dave and then they picked up the girls, Arlene and Mildred. Bernard and Mildred hit it off, and eventually married.

CHAPTER 9

Mabel

IT WAS 1925. WHILE FANNY was finishing up a card reading for a client, Loretta and May were watching the store for her. Henrietta had gone to visit her friend Belle Whitman, and Sylvia and Bernard were playing outside. Mabel was busy sewing in the back of the house. She loved to sew, and was very good at it. Fanny figured she took after her sister Anna in that way. All of a sudden Mabel felt a pain in her lower right side. She didn't think much about it at first. Maybe it was indigestion or maybe she had strained a muscle. She kept on sewing. By and by, the pain came on stronger. She felt the area of the pain with her hands. There was a tender spot. When she released her hand it seemed to hurt even more.

Mabel decided to go lie down and wait for the pain to pass. She went to her bed, and when she got there the pain was unbearable.

"Mama, Mama," she cried out.

Fanny rushed in to see what was happening.

"What's the matter, Mabel?"

"Mama, I don't feel well. I have a terrible pain in my right side."

"Lie down. I'll get you something to eat."

"No, Mama, I'm not hungry," she replied.

"Just rest, then. You will probably feel better in the morning. Let's wait and see. I'll bring you some peppermint tea."

After lying down Mabel continued to have pain. Later, as the pain subsided, she began to feel dizzy and nauseous. She quickly got a fever and chills. Fanny covered her with lots of blankets. When the other girls came home, they began to worry. May was particularly upset that her twin sister was so sick.

"Mama, call the doctor!" they all said with alarm.

Fanny called Dr. Weidenthal, who came right over and examined her. He thought she might have caught the flu, so he gave her some medicine and asked Fanny to call him in the morning. Mabel didn't seem to improve, and in fact continued to get worse. Fanny was worried sick.

When Henrietta returned from Belle's house and learned of her sister's illness, she went to the kitchen to make dinner for Sylvia and Bernard and then helped them prepare for bed.

"Mabel will be better in the morning," she assured them, even though in her heart she wasn't really sure.

After the children were sleeping, Henrietta went to Mabel's bedside. By this time Mabel was so sick she couldn't even raise her head. She felt heavy, feverish, and nauseous.

The four women gathered around Mabel in utter distress. When it was apparent she was not improving, May pleaded, "Mama, we have to take Mabel to the hospital!" But at this point Mabel was too sick to move.

"Mama," she whispered softly, turning toward Fanny, "I love you." As Fanny put her hand on Mabel's forehead, Mabel said, "Don't blame yourself."

She turned to May, "May, don't be sad. I will always be with you, guiding you. You are like my own soul. I will live on in you."

Turning to Loretta, she uttered, "Loretta, take care of everyone, especially Bernard. Help him throughout his life. Don't let him fall. May Henrietta and Sylvia be happy."

Mabel felt like she was beginning to fade away. The intense pain had forced her awareness outside of her body, so that she no longer experienced it and no longer felt sick. She began to feel light, as though she were hovering over her body.

"Mama," she barely spoke, "tell Papa I miss him, and that I will see him soon."

With great love, she took a long look at her mama and each of her sisters. She radiated a special love and gratitude for May—with whom she had begun this journey in the same womb—and for Mama and Papa, who enabled them to come together into this world.

"Open the window," Fanny told Henrietta.

Mabel then closed her eyes and slipped away.

CHAPTER 10

Mabel's Funeral

THE WOMEN STAYED BY MABEL'S side the rest of the night, heartbroken. No one wanted to move from that spot.

In accord with Jewish custom, as an expression of the pain of the passing of a loved one, and as a symbol that the body is only a covering for the indwelling soul, Fanny tore her blouse. Under her breath she recited:

Böruch atöh adonöy, בָּרוּךְ אַתָּה יְיָ,

elohay-nu melech hö-olöm, אֱלֹהֵינוּ מֶלֶךְ הָעוֹלָם,

da-yan hö-emes. דַּיַּן הָאֱמֶת:

"Blessed art Thou, O Lord our God, King
of the Universe, the true Judge."

"Loretta, run and get your Papa," Fanny said in the early hours of the next morning.

Hyman came running over after he got the news.

"Fanny, what's happened? What's happened to Mabel?"

"She's gone, Hyman," Fanny cried, as she put her head on his shoulder. They remained embraced in a pool of grief for some time.

They called the doctor to come over. He examined Mabel and determined she had sepsis from a burst appendix. He called the coroner, who came by to examine the body and prepare the death certificate. The coroner arranged for the transport of the body to the Jewish funeral home, which was next to the Temple, while Fanny and Hyman arranged the funeral. May accompanied Mabel to the funeral home to sit by her body. According to Jewish law it was not permitted for the body to be left alone until the burial. Hyman and Loretta went to the Euclid Avenue Temple to speak with Rabbi Eliezer.

"*Shalom.* Welcome, what may I do for you?" the Rabbi spoke.

"With a very heavy heart I am here to say that Mabel has died," Hyman blurted out through his tears. "We need to plan her funeral to take place as soon as possible."

As the Rabbi spoke, tears welled up in his eyes. "I am deeply sorry to hear of this. She was a beautiful girl, so full of life, so talented. We can arrange for the funeral to take place tomorrow at ten in the morning."

Henrietta was in charge of getting Bernard's breakfast the next day. Bernard was scared when he woke up and heard that his beloved sister, Mabel, was dead. Fanny sent a note with a neighbor to Sylvia and Bernard's school, explaining that the children would be absent for the rest of the week due to a death in their family.

Hyman and his parents arranged for the casket and flowers, and made sure everything was in order for the funeral the next day. While his parents were making arrangements, Bernard just wanted to run away. He was only seven years old. He didn't understand fully what had happened, but he knew he didn't want to be home. He ran outside and stayed outside that whole day. He wandered along the nearby Dome Creek, picking up stones and throwing them in the water and watching the surface of the water ripple.

Hyman's parents came over to help, so Fanny wouldn't have to think about all the arrangements for the funeral. Fanny covered all the mirrors and lit a mourner's candle and placed it on the table. She unlocked the front door and placed a pitcher of water just outside the entryway, so those entering the home could wash their hands. She was preparing to "sit *shiva*"—the Jewish custom of grieving at home and receiving guests—for seven days from the day after the funeral took place. Everyone was in shock and was despondent that day. No one talked very much.

The funeral took place the next day. Mabel was laid in a simple pine casket, clothed in one of her favorite blue dresses. Wisps of her soft brown hair spread out on the pillow upon which her head rested. Her mouth was slightly curved, as if she were gently smiling. She looked like a sleeping angel.

All were allowed to view the body before the service—Fanny, the girls, Hyman and his family. The open casket had been placed on the stage, behind an imposing dark red velvet curtain. Solemnly, one by one, they paid their last respects. There were lots of tears and enormous sadness. Fanny felt a stabbing pain in her heart that she knew would never heal. Then she looked around for Bernard.

"Sylvia," Fanny said, "Where is Bernard? Please, go get Bernard."

Bernard was outside, hiding behind a tree. He didn't want anything to do with this death business. When Sylvia found him, he was scared and shivering.

"Come on, Bernard. Mama wants you." She led Bernard into the Temple, to where Fanny was sitting.

"Here he is," she told her mama, as Sylvia presented her baby brother to her.

Fanny took Bernard by the arm. He let out a yell.

"Bernard," she told him, "I want you to say good-bye to your sister Mabel." Together they approached the stage. Bernard was squirming, afraid of what he might find behind that mysterious dark velvet curtain that separated life from death.

"No, no, no. Please, Mama. No, no, no," he cried out.

Fanny told Bernard to look at his sister and say good-bye. She explained to him that this was the last time he would ever see her. He didn't understand. And besides, he was just too scared to look at the body. He turned away. Determined that her son would have one last look at his sister, Fanny grabbed hold of his face, one hand on each cheek, and turned his head—forcing him to look at Mabel. When she let go of him, he screamed and ran out of the Temple. He ran all the way home and hid in his room.

"Let him go," Hyman said. "He's just a young boy."

Everyone took their seats, and the funeral service began with the *Kaddish,* the Jewish prayer recited by mourner's following the death of a loved one.

"Magnified and Sanctified, holy be Thy Name in this world created according to Divine Will . . ."

Yit-ga-dal ve-yit-ka desh sh'may rabba, b'alma dee vera chir-ootay . . . the Rabbi started.

". . . And May the One who makes peace in the heavens make peace for all of us, and for all of Israel, and for the whole world, and let us say Amen."

After the service, the funeral party followed the gravediggers to the graveyard in the back of the Temple. Rabbi Eliezer said a few words as the casket was lowered into the ground. And so Mabel was put to final rest.

For months after Mabel died, Fanny walked around in a daze. She couldn't accept her daughter's death. When she would think of her beloved Mabel, her throat closed, her heart felt heavy, and tears spilled down her cheeks. She vividly remembered Mabel's last words to her, urging her not to blame herself, but it was so hard not to. It was a trying time for everyone. Her twin sister May felt incredibly lonely. Never before, not even once, had she been without Mabel.

As time passed, life went on. May married and left the house. Loretta met Joe and opened her own store and café a few blocks away from Fanny's. By the end of the decade, Henrietta was married. And by the early 1930s, so was Sylvia.

CHAPTER 11

Brownie and the Bootleggers

IN 1920 THE VOLSTEAD ACT passed. This made the sale and consumption of liquor illegal all across the United States. As this seemed so outrageous at the time, very few people actually stopped drinking. In fact, a large black market for liquor rapidly developed. It became a lucrative business opportunity for the gangsters. There were two big mobs in Cleveland: the Mayfield Road Mob, headed by Frank Milano; and the Lonardo family, headed by Big Joe. The headquarters for the Milano gang was the Little Italy restaurant located in the Italian section of Mayfield Road. Frank's gang was involved with dealing in corn sugar, which was used in the private stills to make liquor. They had a big Syndicate that involved corn growers, processors, and stills throughout Cleveland and the Ohio countryside. The members of the Syndicate would bring corn whiskey into the city and sell it to the Bootleggers through a series of associates.

No one really liked Prohibition—and Fanny, like many people in those days, saw selling liquor as an opportunity to support her large family. By now she knew just about everyone in the city, including the policemen. So she contacted a customer of hers, whose cousin was Sammy Wakovich. He knew an associate with the Mayfield Gang who operated a still; they offered Fanny the opportunity to buy liquor in large quantities to sell undercover and illegally in her store. The stills were tucked away in barns and basements. Some individuals made "bathtub gin," but mostly the growing and distilling of liquor was done through the Syndicate. Liquor flowed everywhere, if you knew where to look. There were "speakeasies," which were nightclubs that sold liquor. They were very popular, but you had to know someone affiliated with one of them and a secret password to get inside the door. You could easily get whisky from the pharmacies just by providing a doctor's prescription, which could be for any number of ailments ranging from depression to anxiety. Sacrificial wine was flowing aplenty at Churches and Synagogues, and the number of congregants grew during this time.

Fanny had a storeroom at the back of her shop. It had a simple table and chairs where she did her card and tea leaf readings. It also had an underground storage cellar where she kept the liquor, which was accessible only by a wooden trapdoor. Fanny placed an old Turkish carpet over the trapdoor. She asked Mabel to sew curtains to cover the windows of the back room, as well as to sew petticoats for her sisters with pockets in them large enough to hold a bottle of whisky. It was 1923. Only Sylvia was too young to participate in this scheme.

Fanny developed a clandestine system. When the men came into the store, they would signal that they wanted a drink by winking their left eye. Fanny would then send two girls to the back room to prepare for the customers. One of them would close the curtains and get out the glasses. The other would open the trapdoor to get out the liquor bottles. They would hide them in the pockets of their petticoats until the men came into the room. While the girls were preparing the room, Fanny collected the money and gave them a ticket. Only then would Fanny send them to the back, where her daughters were waiting with the bottles under their skirts. When the men came in and presented their tickets, the girls would lift their skirts to remove the bottles and pour the customers a drink. A table and chairs were in the room so they could sit while drinking. Fanny made sure there was more than one girl in the room at all times, for safety. She didn't want the men to get fresh or take extra liberties with her daughters. Of course, the men would try to strike up a conversation, and the girls were taught to be polite, but not to say too much.

Around this time Fanny had a dog, a water spaniel named Brownie, who was trained to growl and bite if provoked or on command. Fanny would send the dog to the back room with the girls for protection, where she would watch with her ears cocked and nose sniffing, as the girls lifted the rug and got out the bottles. She knew the routine. The girls got out the bottles from the trapdoor, and the men came into the room to drink. Brownie stood on guard and alert. She certainly understood her job as a watchdog!

Mabel and May were a little shy and didn't like lifting their skirts in front of the men. Loretta was tough. She knew this was necessary for the survival of the family. She would give the men a mean look as if to say, "*Don't try anything*," and would have a growling dog by her side as if to say, "*I mean business*." If she didn't know the customer, she carried a gun with her into the back room. Henrietta, who was the youngest, was the most affected. By nature she was flirtatious, but on her own terms. She was embarrassed and humiliated by this familial duty. Most of the men were repeat customers and friends of Fanny. Very few were total strangers. This went on throughout the 1920s.

One day Fanny was at the back of the store writing up weekly orders when the phone rang. She got up from her table and walked to the front of the store to answer.

"Is this Mrs. Fanny Shaw?" an authoritative man's voice bellowed.

"Yes," she replied hesitantly.

"This is Officer O'Malley. We have reports that you are serving liquor at your store. We are coming over to investigate."

Fanny hung up the phone and went to the back room to put everything away into the hidden cellar. She cleared out the glasses and opened the curtains to let the light in. By now Fanny knew the policemen, and they always warned her before coming over.

Within five minutes there was a forceful knock at the door. Fanny opened the door.

"Good afternoon, Officer O'Malley. What can I do for you?"

"We're here to search the place for illegal liquor. We had some reports of illicit activity going on in your store."

"Help yourself," Fanny said, confident that everything would turn out alright.

The officers walked around the premises, trying their best not to find anything.

"We can't find anything," they said with a wink.

Fanny slipped them a $5 bill as they left, and thanked them for coming. Fanny knew the local policemen, so she wasn't too worried. Most of them were customers who stopped by the store for a soda or a pack of cigarettes. Some of their wives had consulted her for various problems. They were all friendly towards her and her five daughters and son. But whenever there was a complaint, the police were obliged to follow up on it.

This went on for a long time. The police would call to warn Fanny before coming, and she'd slip them a $5 bill as they were leaving. And Fanny would continue to sell liquor that she bought from the Mayfield Gang mafia. They delivered the bottles to her in crates that were labeled Mustard and Ketchup. It was always delivered C.O.D. Fanny always had the money to pay.

Little Bernard would get scared when the police came, so Fanny would send him out to play on these occasions. If he saw the police car in front of the store, he'd run away, and he wouldn't come home until the police left. He didn't understand what was going on, but he didn't want to be caught by the policemen. He was always worried for his mama that she might be sent to jail. Then what would he do?

One fine day came when, as usual, the police called to warn Fanny they were coming. Brownie was following Fanny around, and went with her into the back room as she put the bottles away in the cellar, opened the curtains, and cleared away the glasses. Brownie sniffed at the cellar door, cocked her ears, and then followed Fanny to the front of the store.

Fanny patted Brownie and gave her a treat. "Good girl," she said as she stroked her back. Brownie proudly wagged her tail.

By-and-by there was a knock at the door. It was the policemen doing their job as usual, protecting the community, and upholding the law.

"We're here to search the place for illegal liquor," they said. "We had some reports of illicit activity going on here."

"Hello, officers. Please help yourselves," Fanny replied, feeling relaxed and certain that things would go as usual. As the officers were looking around, Fanny continued to work and sold a bottle of Coca Cola and a Hershey's chocolate bar to a customer who had come into the store.

The officers walked around the premises, trying their best not to find anything. But this time, as they were looking around, Brownie, who was feeling pretty good about herself, thought these men had come for a drink. She barked and barked as she ran back and forth towards the back room, as if she wanted them to follow her. The policemen followed her into the back room. Then Brownie barked and barked, and sniffed at the trapdoor as if to say, *"Here it is!"* So the officers felt compelled to look under the Turkish rug, and there they found the trapdoor. When they lifted the trapdoor, they found a stash of whisky that they immediately confiscated.

"Mrs. Shaw," they said, "We will have to take you down to the station and book you for illegal possession of alcohol."

The officers handcuffed Fanny and put her in the back of their paddy wagon. They took her down to the station, where they booked her for possession of alcohol. Fanny was stunned. She hadn't expected the inspection to go wrong.

"Darn that Brownie," she thought to herself. *"She's so smart! But her cleverness gave us away!"*

After a lot of paperwork and a lot of waiting, Fanny asked to see Lieutenant Herman Goldman. Lieutenant Goldman was the son of Molly's friend, for whom she had done a card reading many years before. Indeed, her son did in fact become a policeman, as she had predicted, and he had been an old friend of the family for many years since then. Fanny appealed to him to be lenient. After much discussion, they finally settled on a fine, and he let her go.

From then on, Fanny had to be a more careful bootlegger.

CHAPTER 12

Hyman

HYMAN HAD BEEN AS GOOD a dad as he could be, considering his wife had thrown him out of the house. He would come and see the children on weekends. When the older girls grew up and they wanted to be with their friends, he would just pick Bernard and Sylvia up and take them out for ice cream or for a sleepover at his apartment. Bernard was uneasy with this arrangement. He would have preferred that his parents were living together. This put him in an embarrassing situation. In those days it was unthinkable for parents to be divorced. At school he had to pretend his parents were still married. Hyman had a lady friend for a while, who had a car. She and Hyman would pick Bernard up and take him for a Sunday drive in the country. He liked that.

Even though they had been divorced, Fanny still had tender feelings for Hyman. He was the father of her children, and he had been a good father. He regularly came by to take the children out and spend time with them, he attended their school functions, and he bought their school supplies and clothes.

Then one day in 1929 Hyman drove to the market and parked his car at the curb. Just as he got out of his car on the street side, another car came by and hit him. Hyman fell to the ground. He was rushed to the hospital, but was dead on arrival. Bernard felt a strange sense of relief, because now he could say his father was dead. And in those days this was a lot more respectable than saying his parents were divorced. It wasn't exactly his fault. His parents had been separated since before he was born, and he never knew what it was like to live with his father. When he got older he sorely regretted those feelings he'd experienced as a child, and wished it had been otherwise.

Hyman's death made Fanny reflect on the importance of family. She was feeling sad for her children that their father had died. She knew that her own father had meant the world to her, and her thoughts turned to her own parents. *How are father and mother doing? Are they still alive? If only I could see them once again.* She wished in all her heart that things had been different between her and Hyman, and that they could have lived a happy life together.

This was the start of a hard year for Fanny and the family. The Great Depression of the 1930s was about to begin.

CHAPTER 13

BB Mason and the Racketeers

AFTER THE STOCK MARKET CRASH of 1929, The Great Depression set in deep throughout the 1930s. Ruin, poverty, and despair struck the heart of the country. Fifteen million people were unemployed, which represented 25% of all American workers! The impact was deeply felt in Cleveland, especially in the poor Jewish and Black neighborhoods. There were food stamps, bread lines, and soup kitchens everywhere. The Volstead Act was repealed in 1933, which made selling liquor no longer illegal.

This was good news for Fanny. She struggled, as everyone did, at the beginning of the Depression. There weren't as many customers as before, but there were fewer mouths to feed. Mabel was gone. May had married Samuel Ganz, and they lived in their own apartment. Loretta had left home to live with Joe, her boyfriend, and opened a café and bar of her own on Central Avenue in East Cleveland. It was just a few blocks away from Fanny's store. By then, Henrietta was married to Ben Zirin, and just Sylvia and Bernard were home. That took a lot of strain off Fanny.

Loretta had met Joe Stowers at Fanny's store. He was a policeman who frequented the store to buy cigarettes. Joe admired Loretta

179

because she was independent and could take care of herself. She knew how to run a business; she could cook and also made good coffee. Besides that, she was streetwise and could handle a gun as good as any man. Her gun was a real *beauty*—a pearl-handled revolver that she kept behind the bar. And she didn't hesitate to pull it out on some drunken, unruly customer when needed!

Joe loved all that about Loretta. She loved Joe too. And since he was on the police force, he offered some protection to their family. Joe wanted to ask Loretta to marry him, but he really could not. He was half German and half Black. And although there were no anti-miscegenation laws in Ohio, there were the unwritten cultural and religious taboos. A Jew could not marry a non-Jew, and certainly not a Black man. And likewise for the Black community, it was frowned upon to marry outside. As a result, they just lived together in the rooms behind the bar. Loretta took his name to pledge their union and their love, and to present an air of respectability.

And so, Loretta ran the café and bar, and Joe patrolled the streets. They had a dog, a standard dull-gray Schnauzer named Joey. Joe trained him to be a guard dog who would snarl and attack on command. As a result, Joey was a mean dog.

Loretta's bar was on Central Avenue in East Cleveland, across from the Warner and Swasey tool factory. The workers would walk over to Loretta's café for a lunch sandwich and a beer. It was a good location. And on payday they would all come over to drink whiskey and eat dinner. There was a counter with barstools, where people would place their orders and drink their beer, and there were tables and chairs in the café. The walls were bare, and the floors had alternating black-and-white square linoleum tiles. The cash register sat on top of a glass case. The top two shelves displayed enticing candy bars and gum. Joey sat on the bottom shelf, growling and snapping menacingly all day long as a warning— just in case anybody got any ideas!

One day, Henrietta was helping Loretta in her bar. It was payday, and all the workers from the Warner and Swasey factory were busy cashing their checks. That day, Loretta had a lot of cash on hand. Suddenly, one of the men who had gathered there pulled out a gun! Pointing it directly at her, he demanded all the money. Joey snarled and barked from inside the glass case. Loretta just ignored the man and turned around to get *her* gun. Seeing this, and fearing for Loretta's safety, Henrietta picked up a beer bottle and threw it over the counter, hitting the robber's hand that was holding the gun. She hit him good, and blood gushed out all over his clothes and onto the floor. Flustered by the sheer audacity of these two women, he turned and ran out of the store.

After the Volstead Act was repealed and liquor became legal again, new Syndicates arose in the city.

Benny Mason, known as BB Mason, became the overlord of the street gambling enterprise known as the "*numbers racket*." They called him the Kingpin of the city's racketeering! During the Depression era of the 1930s, the numbers racket was an illegal betting system that took over the streets of Cleveland with a vengeance. It was especially popular in the poor neighborhoods. Betting on the numbers offered a chance to make a buck.

The numbers racket went like this:

Gamblers would place bets with a *bookie*, at a tavern or private place, by choosing three numbers from 1 to 999. The bookies sent the money and bets through a *runner* to the *policy writers*. The policy writers collected the bets and handed the money off to the Kingpin. The Kingpin, in turn, would pick the numbers at random on a specified day and then broadcast the winning numbers to the policy writers.

The bookies kept 10% of the money they collected, and had to split that with the runner. Depending on how much they collected, bookies could make a decent amount of money. The policy writers did even better, as they kept 25% of all the bets they collected from many bookies. The Kingpin, who of course ran the racket, paid 500:1 to the gamblers—which left him with about 15% of all the gambling money collected.

Money was constantly pouring in from every street corner in the city. All of this illegal activity took place at the B&M Policy House on East 46th Street. This is where the bets were received and paid out.

During the Depression, Fanny saw this as a good way to make money for the family and to keep her store running. She collected bets and sent Bernard to run them to the policy writers. She sewed a pocket on the inside of his pants to carry the money.

"Bernard, be careful on the streets," she would tell him. "Do not stop and talk to anyone until the money is delivered! You must promise me this."

"Okay, Mama," he replied. "I promise." By this time, Bernard was a teenager. He loved the feeling of freedom he felt when he walked down the street with all the money hidden in his pants pocket. Fanny wasn't worried. She knew Bernard was a good boy.

He was also recruited to run bookings for his big sister Loretta from her bar on Central Avenue. This kept him busy after school and on the weekends. Loretta always paid him in chocolate bars, and he had the pick of all the candy and gum he wanted from inside her glass counter.

About this time, Ben Zirin, Henrietta's husband, was having a rough time. He drank and gambled too much. He'd stay out all night and womanize too often, even after his daughter Myra was born. He'd hang out at his sister-in-law Loretta's bar, and there he would place bets on the numbers. It seemed innocent enough to Loretta, who collected bets all day long.

Ben had a run-in at Benny Mason's Farm, the Kingpin's suburban nightclub. Ben had drunk and gambled a little too much. He owed $500, and BB was calling in the debt. He sent one of his henchmen, Bobby Longlegs, to seek him out.

"Zirin," he shouted while waving his gun, "BB wants his money. He's calling in your debt. It's due in three days. If you don't pay up, you'll be at the bottom of the lake on day four!"

"Bobby," he pleaded, "I don't have it. What am I going to do?"

"BB doesn't care. Do whatever you got to, but have the money in three days and deliver it to The Farm . . . or else!"

Ben was paralyzed with fear. There was no way he could get that kind of money in three days—or ever. He ran and ran around the city, sweating, nervous, and exhausted. He knew he was a marked man. He couldn't go to Henrietta. She was fed up with him and was even thinking of filing for divorce!

Late that night, out of desperation Ben ran to his sister-in-law Loretta's bar. He knew she kept a loaded revolver behind the counter, and he knew exactly where she kept it. Fraught with fear and distress, he ran into the bar when Loretta was in the back of the store. Luckily for him, Joey was out in the backyard, relieving himself and sniffing around. So he grabbed the gun, ran down to the basement, and went over to the coal furnace, which was burning hot. He breathed in a sigh of desperation, put the gun to his head and pulled the trigger. He breathed out a sigh of relief as he fell to the ground.

Joey and Loretta heard the noise. They ran down to the basement, but it was too late. Ben lay lifeless in a pool of blood.

Loretta was helpless. As Joey sniffed at Ben's body, she ran upstairs to call Joe at the police station. She asked him to come home right away with a detective and an ambulance. The ambulance came and carted the body to the morgue. The detective came to make a report. Loretta's gun became evidence in the crime, and she had to get a new one after that.

Ben and Henrietta's daughter, Myra, was only two years old at the time of his suicide. When Myra was a little older, Loretta thought it would be a good idea to show her niece where her father had died. So one day she brought the little girl down to the basement near the furnace, to show her the place where her father had shot himself. Although Myra was only seven years old at the time, she would always remember her Aunt Loretta showing her the spot near the furnace and laughing cynically, as if to say: *Look at what that damn fool did!*

CHAPTER 14

Desperate Measures
for Desperate Times

As the Great Depression wore on, life got harder and harder. By the mid-1930s, only Bernard was living at home with Fanny. She had fallen on hard times and was about to lose her store. Right about then, she heard from Jack Bernstein, a client for whom she had done tea leaf readings. Jack had a distant cousin named Johnny Dunman, who was about to lose his house due to foreclosure. In a last, desperate attempt to save Johnny's investment in it, Jack asked Fanny if she'd help his cousin out a little.

To make it look like he was going to get income from the house to pay the mortgage, Johnny would make up a lease for Fanny to sign. Fanny and Bernard would then move into the house for just a little while. And when the time came, he would call Fanny at the store and tell her not to go home that night with her son. Fanny seriously considered the proposal. She even consulted a tea leaf reading for herself to see if it was a good idea to participate in this scheme. In the end, there was money in it for Fanny, so she agreed.

"Bernard," Fanny told him one day, "we're going to move into Johnny Dunman's house for a while. Just bring one suitcase of clothes and a toothbrush."

Fanny and Bernard packed their suitcases, and proceeded to move into the house. There were beds in the two bedrooms and utensils in the kitchen. The living room had an old sofa, with the springs popping out, and a dusty old radio. Bernard was glad for the radio. He liked to listen to weekly programs such as *The Lone Ranger* and *The Shadow*. *"Only the Shadow knows . . ."*

Fanny liked to listen to *The Jack Benny Show* and *Burns and Allen*. And it was good to listen to FDR's fireside chats on Sunday nights, for the President had a soothing voice that calmed the nerves of the nation.

Bernard was attending Glenville High School at this time, and he kept up his routine of driving Fanny to the store in the morning and then going to school. This went on for several weeks.

One day, Fanny got the call from Johnny, advising her not to go home to sleep that night. After school, when Bernard picked Fanny up, she told him to pack his suitcase, as they were going to spend the night at his sister May's house. Bernard was happy about this, for he liked playing with his young nephew Matthew.

To Bernard's surprise, in the morning news there were reports of a large explosion at the house in East Cleveland where they had been living! There was extensive damage. Fortunately, no one was at home. The insurance adjusters investigated the incident, and they deemed it an accident even though they were suspicious of foul play. The gas tank had exploded. The police called Bernard down to the station to question him about the explosion, but he didn't know anything. Fanny hadn't told him. In the end, Johnny Dunman received $5,000 cash from his insurance company, of which Fanny received $500. This little infusion of cash helped Fanny to stay afloat in her store for a little while longer after that.

CHAPTER 15

Out on the Street

DURING THE 1920S FANNY HAD a customer who was a real estate agent. He encouraged her to buy various properties. But during the Depression her tenants couldn't pay the rent, and she was left with a lot of debt. In 1936, Bernard was the only child left at home. He had finished high school and was working in a factory, checking industrial metal buckets for leaks. His sister Loretta had gotten him that job. Times were tough. When his shoes got holes in them, he'd just put cardboard across the holes and keep on walking.

Fanny had temporarily lost her store. She moved into one of the properties she owned, which the tenants had moved out of. They stayed there for a while. But when the first of the month came along, Fanny could not pay the rent. This went on for a couple of months. One day, the sheriff came to her door and forcefully knocked on it. At this time Fanny had a small dog, Nellie, who barked loudly when she smelled and heard someone at the door.

"It's the Cuyahoga County Sheriff!" he shouted. "Open up in the name of the law!"

Nellie started to snarl when she heard this, and her barking became even louder.

"Quiet!" she told her dog. "I'm just as distressed as you, but please be quiet!" She held Nellie back.

"Yes," she shouted to the man, "I'm coming." Fanny feared the worst, and her heart skipped a beat as she opened the door.

"You are in default of paying your rent. The bank is calling in your loan. You must pay or else leave! You have ten days to get out."

Nellie snarled again as the door shut behind the man. Fanny patted her. "I feel the same way you do, girl, but we'll both just have to get through this."

Fanny was upset, but she tried to put it all out of her mind. She just kept living in the house. She didn't tell Bernard that the house was being foreclosed. They didn't really have any other place to go. Fanny worried about losing the house, but these were hard times for everybody. She was no longer able to pay the mortgage on her store, and very few people were able to pay for fortune-telling.

One day, Bernard was at home listening to the radio while Fanny was cooking lunch in the kitchen. Nellie was following her around, looking for crumbs to eat that might drop on the floor. Suddenly there was a gruff knock at the door.

"It's the Cuyahoga County Sheriff!" the voice shouted. "We are here with a warrant for the removal of your household goods!"

They busted the door in. "Are you Mrs. Shaw?"

"Yes," she replied anxiously.

"Cleveland Savings and Loan, the owner of this property, has foreclosed this house due to failure to pay the mortgage. We're moving everything out into the street."

The Sheriffs went about removing all of Fanny's furniture and setting it onto the sidewalk. First they grabbed the sofa, and then came the table and chairs, the beds, the lamps, and the radio. They proceeded to take everything from the kitchen, putting the utensils, pots, and mixing bowls in a box and setting them on the kitchen table, which they had placed outside. Finally, they even removed the stove—coal still burning in it!—and set it outside on the sidewalk.

It took them several hours to get everything out. Fanny and Bernard just watched helplessly. When everything was stacked outside, Nellie sniffed at the pile of furniture and household goods, then cocked her head and whimpered as though recapturing familiar nostalgic smells.

"Mama!" Bernard complained. "What's going on?"

What could Fanny say? The Depression had defeated her. It had taken her store and her home. Fanny was down, but not out. Being resourceful, she could pick herself up again—and she would!

Bernard was so embarrassed, but there was nothing he could do. Fanny did the only thing she could. She put up a sign right there on the street: 'Yard Sale – Everything Must Go'.

Some passersby bought a few things. When it got dark, it was time to leave.

"Come on, Bernard. We'll spend the night at your sister Loretta's."

They turned around and left everything right there on the sidewalk. And as they walked on down the street, Nellie followed close behind—with her ears down and her tail between her legs.

CHAPTER 16

The War Years

ON MAY 1, 1938, BERNARD married Mildred Cowan. Although they had met in high school, they waited to marry until Bernard could get a secure job. This was a difficult thing to do during this time. Finally, he was hired by the U.S. Post Office to sort mail on the night shift. It was a monotonous job, but it was steady work. It paid well and had good benefits. He worked there until he was drafted in early 1945, while WWII was still being fought.

By the 1940s, all of Fanny's children were married and had left the house. She no longer owned a store. She rented a small room in a boarding house for herself. The Second World War was raging. News reports of the Jewish concentration camps in Europe alarmed Fanny. She was deeply worried for her family back home and for her friends in Germany who had helped her to come to America. It pained her to think about it. She prayed for their protection.

During this time her fortune-telling business had picked up a little. With the war going on, young men and boys were sent abroad to fight. Many wives and girlfriends were frightened they would never see their loved ones again. They needed some reassurance, and they would consult Fanny with their concerns.

She was grateful that for now Bernard was safe from the draft, since the Army was initially drafting only single men. And by the time America entered the war—when the Army would soon be drafting married men with no children—Bernard and Mildred had a daughter, Marilyn. And then, during the war, they had a son, Jerry.

Loretta kept her bar and café in East Cleveland until the 1970s. After Joe died, she rented one of the rooms in the back of her store to a good friend of Joe's, named Chief. Chief was an African American retired policeman who had been born in slavery. He offered some company and protection for Loretta, and he became like one of the family.

May and Sam had three boys: Matthew, Howard, and Jack. Henrietta had remarried. She and her second husband, Harry, had a daughter they named Marlene. As time went on, though, it turned out that he drank too much and also womanized. When Henrietta found out that Harry was going around with the florist's wife, she divorced him. But she had two daughters to raise, and her sister May also needed a place for her family to live. So it was that the three of them pooled their resources and bought a duplex together on Edgewood Drive in Cleveland Heights. Henrietta and her two daughters lived on the top floor; May and Sam and their sons lived on the bottom floor.

In the house there was an attic room, where Fanny was invited to live after the war. The attic was hot in the summer and cold in the winter. For ventilation it had two small windows, one on each end, and a wooden floor that creaked when she walked across it. Fanny had to climb the stairs to her room, and this increasingly got harder and harder for her. She would spend her days at her daughter May's home on the first floor.

By now, Fanny was older and getting tired. Her heart was giving out. At times, she reflected on the many twists and turns of her life. First she thought fondly of her own childhood and of her family back in the old country. She missed them terribly, and many times had wished they could have met again. She reflected on her teachers, Kalisara and Mrs. Rosenthal, who were so dear to her heart. They had taught her how to develop her intuition, providing her with skills to earnestly help others while earning a supplementary income for herself. Smiling, she thought about Esther, a fitting student who would carry on the tradition of card reading that Fanny had learned in a faraway time and place. She thought too about her brother Arthur, and how he had helped her to come to America.

She fondly remembered Hyman and those early days when they were in love. She sorely regretted how it ended and wished she hadn't been so rash. She thought of all the stores she had operated over the years and of raising her six children. She cried upon thinking of Mabel's untimely death, and how her life had been unfairly snatched away at such a young age.

Fanny knew that over the years she'd been a good business woman and mother, resourceful and tough when she had to be, but also compassionate and tender when called for. She was grateful that all her children were now married, and was glad for the rich blessings of being a grandmother to her seven wonderful grandchildren.

For a moment, she closed her eyes and took a deep breath, touching the unchanging, eternal presence within. And, although a whole lifetime had passed by, it seemed to Fanny as if no time had really passed at all.

AFTERWORD

FANNY DIED IN THE HOSPITAL on March 3, 1949. The cause of death was a heart attack. It was five months before I was born, but I know she knew that I, her last grandchild, was coming. Papa said that her final words were words of thanks. She thanked the doctors for all they did, and then she suddenly died. I would like to think that in the sense of gratitude she expressed at the moment of her death—in her last breath—she was thanking God for her family, for all the good and hard times, for her love of adventure, for her gifts of fortitude in adversity, and for the fullness of life she lived.

I am sorry I never met her, but it seems her love of the hidden mysteries passed on to me. Over the years, I have often felt her presence within, urging me on to unfold my own spiritual endeavors. And for that, I am wholeheartedly grateful to her.

When I began writing my grandmother's story, my motivation was that I wanted to meet her. By the time I finished the project, however, our souls had become so entwined that I began to think: *Maybe, just maybe, she wanted to meet me too!*

In the holy act of Remembering, every man and
woman has a story worth telling.

A C K N O W L E D G E M E N T

I WANT TO THANK MY father, Bernard Shaw, for vividly remembering his colorful childhood. I am also grateful to my husband, Richard Bloedon, for providing enthusiastic encouragement and fine skills in editing and preparing the manuscript; to my brother, Jerry Shaw, for proofreading the text; and to my cousin, Marlene Holderman, for the hours of telephone conversations during which we discussed family stories. I also wish to acknowledge my mother, Mildred Shaw, who would be proud of me—as mothers always are.

AUTHOR'S NOTE

PART I OF THIS STORY is historical fiction, a creative rendering of what might have been. Part II includes accounts of actual events that took place as related to me by my father.

REFERENCES

1. *The World of our Fathers: The Journey of the East European Jews to America and the Life they Found and Made*, Irving Howe, Schocken Books, 1989.
2. *It's All in the Cards*, Chita Lawrence, Berkeley Publishing Group, 1999.
3. Written notes, verbal accounts, and videotaped recordings of my father, Bernard Shaw, recounting stories of his childhood.
4. Unpublished written accounts of life in the Jewish *shtetl* by Samuel Ganz, who was my uncle.
5. *The Encyclopedia of Cleveland*, website maintained by Case Western Reserve University: http://ech.cwru.edu/

Made in the USA
Monee, IL
13 December 2023

49227259R00125